writing
term
papers

writing term papers

the research paper & the critical paper

hulon willis

LATE OF BAKERSFIELD COLLEGE

harcourt brace jovanovich, inc.

NEW YORK   CHICAGO   SAN FRANCISCO   ATLANTA

ISBN: 0-15-598281-8

Library of Congress Catalog Card Number: 76-29189

Printed in the United States of America

preface

Writing Term Papers is a concise guide to writing undergraduate term papers. I have organized the chapters and their components so that students can use the book with a minimum of help from their instructors. With this important goal foremost in my mind, I have endeavored to write with clarity and simplicity and to provide an abundance of pertinent examples to illustrate each aspect of term-paper writing. In short, my aim has been to provide a complete but uncluttered textbook.

Although research and critical papers have important differences, the procedures of writing the two types so overlap that both can be taught effectively in one unified textbook. If students read Chapter 1 (The Nature of Term Papers) with care, they will be able to organize their study of the remainder of the book according to the type of term paper they plan to write. For example, a student writing a critical paper may make less use of Chapter 4 (Library and Other Source Materials) and Chapter 5 (The Working Bibliography) than will a student writing a research paper.

In Chapter 7 (Documentation), I have followed the *MLA Style Sheet.* I have prepared clearly labeled examples of all the forms a student is likely to need. Like experienced writers of term papers or learned articles, who often check footnote and bibliographic forms, students will find it more convenient to verify the correct form when composing an entry than to try to memorize each form.

Because this is a term-paper textbook and not one in composition, I have not included instruction in usage, sentence structure, and paragraph development. Chapter 9 (Writing the Paper) does give instruction in paragraph unity and coherence, however. I have emphasized these two aspects of paragraph composition because, by nature, term papers are particularly subject to paragraphing weak in unity and coherence. Term papers often require students to incorporate in one paragraph materials gathered from several sources. In combining the various materials students often write disjointed sentences and insufficiently related paragraphs. My hope is that Chapter 9 will lead students to compose unified and coherent paragraphs in their term papers. The last part of Chapter 9 presents a complete checklist of both important and minor aspects of preparing the finished paper.

The Appendix (Writing and Documenting the Scientific Term Paper) describes aspects of preparing a scientific term paper and lists examples of reference forms for such disciplines as anthropology, biology, chemistry, mathematics, physics, and psychology.

H. W.

contents

contents

2 topics for research and critical papers 7

3 preliminary reading and outlining 19

4 library and other source materials 23

5 the working bibliography 39

6 note-taking 47

7 documentation 59

contents

writing term papers

1
the nature
of term papers

Term papers are a vital part of the educational process because they require of students intensive study of a limited topic.   In four years of college, a student may write one to two dozen term papers, and often a student's grade in a course is determined chiefly by the quality of the term paper.   Thus it is important for beginning college students to learn the standardized process of writing term papers.   Though standardized, the process is complicated enough to require considerable time and effort to learn, but is not so standardized as to be completely mechanical; it does demand that students learn to exercise judgment.   As students become more experienced in writing term papers, they may develop special techniques of their own.   But to begin with, students must learn basic techniques.   This short text explains and illustrates those techniques in detail.

2   Term papers fall into two broad categories: (1) the research paper (sometimes called the reference paper or the library paper) and (2) the critical paper. Though there are important differences between the two, the basic techniques of preparing them so overlap that both kinds can be taught together in one unified textbook. In the freshman composition course or in one term of it, where instruction in writing term papers is usually given, students may write either a research paper or a critical paper, but they should learn the general techniques that apply to both so that in future courses they will have the ability to write the kind of paper their instructor assigns. We will begin this training by explaining the nature of both the research paper and the critical paper.

THE RESEARCH PAPER

Like many words in English, *research* has more than one meaning. In one sense, it can mean using library source materials to seek out recorded information which is public knowledge. Through such research one may learn, for example, the number and duration of the marriages of John Milton or the content of a particular "Nixon tape" from the Watergate scandals. Or *research* can mean the process of discovering new knowledge—that is, knowledge that has previously been unknown or that, if known before, has been ignored for a long time. Typical results of such research are, for example, the discovery of a new method of synthesizing a hormone or the discovery of a relationship between an eighteenth-century travel book and "The Rime of the Ancient Mariner" by Samuel Taylor Coleridge.

Research that uses source materials to seek out recorded, public knowledge that for the researcher happens to be new may properly be called *practical* research. Research that establishes knowledge new for everyone may properly be called *original* research. In writing term papers, students generally engage in practical research. New knowledge is usually discovered by highly trained researchers in universities, in government, and in industry. Advanced graduate students in universities sometimes engage in productive original research, but they get their start by doing practical research to write term papers.

Though in writing a research paper you will undertake only practical research—the seeking out of recorded knowledge—your finished product should, ideally, be new and original in the sense that the information you gather from various sources will be interpreted in a way never done before. You may put in your paper your own conclusions, based on your study of a topic (though usually other people will have drawn similar conclusions). For example, your research topic might be

"Evolution of Literary Critics' Evaluation of Faulkner's *The Sound and the Fury* Between 1929 and 1946." What critics wrote about *The Sound and the Fury* during those years is recorded, public knowledge. But perhaps no one has investigated that knowledge to determine whether some critics did undergo changes of opinion during those years and, if so, what the nature of these changes was. In your research you will first read as many reviews of the novel as you can find that appeared not long after the novel's publication in 1929. Your notes will record the critical reception of the novel. Then you will seek out a suitable number of articles about the novel that were published after 1929 but before 1947. Your notes will record any changes in the critics' evaluation of the novel. You will then assemble your information into a research paper, which in all probability will be different from any article ever written before. You have engaged in practical research, but you have presented recorded knowledge from a new viewpoint, and in that sense your work is original. Be sure to note that in this hypothetical research paper you yourself would not pass judgment on the quality of *The Sound and the Fury*—that would be a critical paper—but you would assemble recorded knowledge in order to inform your readers as to how critics changed their evaluation of *The Sound and the Fury*. You might, however, philosophize a little on how critical appraisal of the quality of a work of fiction can change dramatically—that would be your own conclusion based on your study of the topic.

Another example will more firmly establish your understanding of the general nature of a research paper. Your topic might perhaps be "Failures in Manned and Unmanned Space Flights During the Last Twenty Years." Though not every failure may be a part of the public record, you can assume, for the sake of writing a college research paper, that the information you need is recorded in your library. You can also safely assume that nobody before has assembled the various pieces of information into one paper. You will begin by seeking out as many instances of failed space flights as possible, taking notes as to where, when, and why the flights failed and the important results of each failure. Then you will assemble your materials into a paper which will present, probably for the first time, a chronological account of important space failures. Since you have sought out only recorded knowledge, you have engaged in practical research. But in a sense you have produced an original work that a great many people might like to read. In addition to assembling recorded information in an original way, you might want to include your own conclusions, based on your study of the topic, as to the chief reasons some space flights failed.

Simply put, then, in writing a research paper you gather from various sources related information (it may come from such sources as personal interviews or television programs as well as from the library) and assemble it into a unified paper that presents the information from a

4   fresh viewpoint.   Students who learn well the process of writing research papers have a great advantage when they are assigned term papers in such disciplines as anthropology, history, literature, psychology, sociology, and so on.   And learning to use the library for practical research can be useful throughout a lifetime.

The steps that constitute the standard method of preparing a research paper—most of which also apply to the critical paper—are explained in their proper order in following chapters.   They are designed to teach eight important aspects of academic work.   First, you are to learn how to do practical research in the library and occasionally in other places.   Such research takes time and perseverance, but the method is standardized and the results are of high educational value.   Second, you are to learn how to take usable notes from your research materials.   In this you must develop much skill, for often only a few sentences in a lengthy article will be relevant to your topic.   You must learn how to spot such information quickly and how to record it on note cards for later use.

Third, you are to learn how to evaluate the validity and reliability of the facts and opinions you gather—how to distinguish between fact and sentiment, scholarship and propaganda.   Fourth, you must learn to digest and assimilate the information your research leads you to.   Do not merely transfer it from the printed page to your note cards without absorbing its content.   Fifth, you are to learn how to interpret the evidence your research uncovers so that you can base sound conclusions on it.   You will, for example, often find contradictory evidence in reputable sources.   For instance, some biographers claim that Lincoln had no religion; others maintain that he was deeply religious.   You must use good judgment in accepting one author's account and rejecting another's.   The whole process of preparing a research paper will help to improve your judgment.

Sixth, you are to learn how to organize your findings, that is, the results of your research, into a unified and coherent paper.   You must learn how to introduce a long paper, how to give its subject matter clear organization, and how to conclude it effectively.   Seventh, you should strengthen your ability to compose effective sentences so that the clear organization you give your paper will have the support of a good expository style.   And eighth, you must learn how to use footnotes and how to list a bibliography so that your paper will be properly documented.   You can learn all of these useful educational devices if you patiently master each step of the standardized procedure of preparing a research paper.

THE CRITICAL PAPER

Criticism, too, has various meanings.   In academic work it refers to the act of making discriminating judgments, evaluations, or interpretations of original creations in the world of art, music, literature, philosophy, the various social sciences, and so on. *Critic* is a noun meaning "one who passes judgment on artistic or intellectual work." Such judgment may be favorable as well as unfavorable. Thus a work of criticism may highly praise rather than find fault with, say, a play by Tennessee Williams. *Critical* is an adjective meaning "pertaining to the act or profession of criticism." As a term paper, therefore, a critical paper contains, in part at least, the student's evaluation or interpretation of some aspect of an author's work. This is its chief difference from a research paper, which may be only a presentation of facts and opinions assembled from various sources.

When assigning critical term papers, most instructors request documentation, a requirement that makes the critical paper and the research paper similar in many respects. Documentation in both the research paper and the critical paper means the acknowledgment of the sources of important information in the paper. Documentation in the critical paper also means the citing of specific passages in an author's work that the student uses as evidence for his or her particular interpretation or evaluation of some aspect of the work. Occasionally, some instructors assign short critical papers without requiring documentation. But in this text we will discuss only the documented critical paper, since that is the kind usually assigned as a term paper.

The source materials for a critical paper may be only primary sources or they may be both primary and secondary. A *primary* source is the original work of an author (or authors) that the critical paper interprets or evaluates. For example, you might choose the topic "Shakespeare's Characterization of Common Soldiers in the History Plays." You might find that no one, so far as your practical research divulges, has written on this particular aspect of Shakespeare's plays. In that case, you will use only primary sources—the history plays themselves—in writing your paper. You will then skip some of the steps necessary in preparing a research paper, but you will take notes, write, and document your critical paper just as you would a research paper. The documentation will cite the specific passages in the plays that you will use as evidence for your interpretation of Shakespeare's attitude toward and use of common soldiers in his history plays.

Secondary sources are writings about an author or about a part of his or her work. Many, if not most, critical term papers make use of both primary and secondary sources, and in this respect they are similar to research papers. For example, in a psychology course you might choose the topic "Contradictions in B. F. Skinner's Philosophy of Determinism as Evidenced in *Beyond Freedom and Dignity*." The one primary source for your paper will be Skinner's book itself. Skinner, however, is a well-known psychologist whose theories and work have been much discussed in popular magazines as well as in scholarly works. In preparing your critical paper, you will investigate, through practical re-

6   search, some secondary sources to see what ideas they can provide to help you make your own interpretation of an aspect of Skinner's book. In writing your paper, you will make your own evaluation of Skinner's philosophic inconsistency, but you are also free to cite secondary sources to bolster your own views. In documenting your paper you will not only cite passages from the primary source but will acknowledge your secondary sources as well.

The work involved in preparing a critical paper is quite similar to that of preparing a research paper. The chief difference is that the critical paper is more likely to require original thought on the part of the student. But, again, the standardized process of preparing each kind of paper is sufficiently similar to allow one unified textbook to teach both kinds of term paper. The following chapters explain and illustrate the standardized process step by step.

2
topics for research and critical papers

PROPERLY LIMITED TOPICS

Sometimes students are provided with properly limited term-paper topics, sometimes they are given general subject areas from which they themselves must derive limited topics, and sometimes they are left completely on their own in choosing topics. Let's assume that you have complete freedom of choice. First, you must understand that a suitable topic for a 2000 to 3000 word term paper must be narrowly limited. No broad or general topic can be treated satisfactorily in only 3000 words. Students have been known to attempt term papers on such topics as "The Napoleonic Wars," "The History of Astrology," or "Political, Economic, and Social Criticism in the Novels of John Steinbeck." Such

8　topics are hopelessly broad, and a paper resulting from one of them is always a hodgepodge of disunified, unsubstantiated generalizations or a series of isolated facts. A good term-paper topic must be limited enough that the resulting paper is unified and has the ring of completeness.

Occasionally a suitably limited topic will just pop into a student's mind. For example, in the first few minutes of a class discussion of term-paper topics a student announced that she wanted to write on "Pollution in New York City in the Decade Preceding the Advent of the Automobile," a good topic for a research paper of 2500 to 3000 words.[1] For some time in the discussion, however, the other students could suggest only broad subject areas, such as "Revolutions in Latin America" and "The Fiction of Ray Bradbury."

Few students, then, can quickly settle on a properly limited topic; most find that they must reduce and reduce and reduce a general topic before they arrive at one suitably limited. Here are some examples of the kind of reducing process you may find necessary:

> *general:* Astronomy
> *less general:* Recent Discoveries in Astronomy
> *more limited:* Information about the Planets Provided by Space Flights
> *properly limited:* Information about Jupiter Provided by Space Flights

> *general:* The Fiction of Ernest Hemingway
> *less general:* Male Characters in the Fiction of Ernest Hemingway
> *more limited:* The Code Hero in the Fiction of Ernest Hemingway
> *properly limited:* The Code Hero in Hemingway's *For Whom the Bell Tolls*

> *general:* Women in Literature
> *less general:* Female Characters in Drama
> *still less general:* Female Characters in Seventeenth-Century Drama
> *more limited:* Female Characters in Molière's Comedies
> *properly limited:* The Independence of Female Characters in Molière's Comedies

---

[1] Of course a whole book could be written on this topic if the author examined all aspects of pollution and was exhaustive in the use of details. Such is the case with most term-paper topics. But the student's suggested topic is still suitably limited for a term paper; in 2000 to 3000 words the topic can be covered in some detail and the paper can be made to sound complete.

general: Transportation
less general: The Advent of the Automobile
still less general: Types of Early Automobiles
more limited: The Steam Automobile
properly limited: The Advantages of Steam Automobiles over
Automobiles with Internal Combustion Engines

The necessity of choosing a narrowly limited topic cannot be overemphasized—remember that you are to write only 2000 to 3000 words, not 200 to 300 pages.

When reducing a broad subject to a limited topic, you may find it helpful to read a general article about that particular field, perhaps in an encyclopedia or magazine. A general article will often contain clues to narrowly limited term-paper topics. For example, one student was interested in writing about an aspect of psychic phenomena—extrasensory perception, telepathy, faith healing, and so on. She found an article entitled "The Present Status of Parapsychology," which was full of generalities and seemed to be of no use. The article, however, made brief mention of an anthropologist skeptical of the existence of psychic phenomena but was cured of a painful leg ailment by a witch doctor. This brief description helped the student to conceive the topic "Skeptical Scientists' Personal Experiences with Psychic Phenomena," and she produced an excellent research paper of about 3000 words.

You must not think, however, that any narrowly limited topic is a good research-paper topic. The chief purpose of a research paper is to teach the student how to assemble pieces of information from various sources—at least ten and sometimes as many as forty—into a unified paper that presents the information from an original viewpoint. Any topic for which you can find sufficient materials in one or two or three sources is not an acceptable research-paper topic, for it will not require you to do a substantial amount of research. For example, suppose you settle on the topic "Early Theories of the Feasibility of Television," which is sufficiently limited and sounds quite interesting. But when you read the article on television in the *Encyclopaedia Britannica* you find that it summarizes all the early theories about the practicality of television. The research has already been done, and you have lost a good topic. Your instructor might agree to let you write on the topic anyway, if you agree to ignore encyclopedia articles and find other sources that are more original. But ideally, you should not choose a research-paper topic that has been fully examined in one published work. In preparing a good research paper, you must engage in detective work, an undertaking that will send you to various sources.

10   FACTUAL AND CONTROVERSIAL TOPICS

A critical paper, since it contains the writer's evaluation or interpretation of some aspect of an author's work, may spark much disagreement among readers who have already formed opinions about the author under discussion. For example, you might write a critical paper entitled "John Steinbeck's *Tortilla Flat* as a Mirror of the Arthurian Round Table," in which you maintain that Steinbeck's novel is intended to show how a once-ideal society decays and dissolves. Another devotee of Steinbeck might object to your thesis, saying that the novel shows how white society damages that of the paisanos. In a sense, then, critical papers are often controversial if read by a number of people. So far as term papers are concerned, however, your instructors will generally be pleased with a well-written critical paper that gives good evidence for its theses.

Research papers present a different problem so far as controversy is concerned. In a critical paper your ideas produce the controversy, but in some research-paper topics the controversy already exists and may have existed for a long time. Of course many research papers are factual and uncontroversial. For example, you might choose the topic "Changes in Laws Relating to Women Within the Last Thirty Years." Your job would be to present a unified, factual account of how such laws changed, not to pass judgment on whether the changes were desirable or undesirable. On the other hand, you might choose the topic "The Equal Rights Amendment: A Social Good or a Social Evil?" Millions of words have been written both praising and condemning this amendment, and your topic would necessarily be controversial. You might simply present major points from both sides and remain neutral; more likely, you would decide that one side presents a better argument and would, after examining the issue, state your own conclusions.

In writing on a controversial topic, however, you should try to be as intellectually honest as possible. Avoid bigoted and propagandistic sources; do not deliberately omit relevant evidence; be careful not to present half-truths or unsubstantiated generalizations; and weigh evidence rationally and calmly. A researcher should be as objective as possible even when dealing with an inflammatory topic, such as an aspect of the conflict between Israel and the Arab countries. Quite often factual proof will be unavailable for the conclusion you draw, but you can present good evidence in a reasonable way. If you do not, the impact of your paper may be weakened considerably.

SUGGESTED TOPICS FOR TERM PAPERS

If you are given freedom of choice in selecting a term-paper topic, one of the following 200 suggestions may interest you. You may want to make changes in a topic, such as in dates covered.

Limited Topics for Research Papers 11

The following fifty topics are sufficiently limited to be suitable research-paper topics:

1 Recent Experiments in Cryogenics (suspending life in low temperatures)
2 Reactions of the Citizens of Asheville, North Carolina, to the Publication in 1929 of Thomas Wolfe's *Look Homeward, Angel*
3 Themes in the Acceptance Speeches of Nobel Prize Winners in Literature
4 Educational Successes (or Failures) in the Busing of School Children to Achieve Integration
5 How Communications Satellites Work
6 Controversy over Diego Rivera's Artistic Work in the United States
7 Social Commentary in the Lyrics of Rock Music in the 1960s
8 The Causes and Outcomes of Professional Football Players' Strikes in the 1970s
9 Social Work Pertaining to the "Battered Child" in the 1960s and 1970s
10 Controversy in the 1970s over Sex Education in the Public Schools
11 The Harmful (Harmless) Effects of Marijuana Reported by Some Researchers
12 Does the Pass-Fail Grading System Affect Student Achievement?
13 Controversy over the Value of Vitamin C in Preventing or Curing the Common Cold
14 How Women's Suffrage Was Established in the Territory of Wyoming
15 State Laws Passed in the 1970s Pertaining to Medical Malpractice
16 The Origin and Early Development of the Detective Story
17 The Rise and Decline of a Particular College Fad
18 A Case for Organically Grown Food
19 The Influence of Religious Music on Jazz
20 The Origin and Early Results of the Head-Start Program
21 The Origin and Early History of Science Fiction
22 Important Activities of the Sierra Club During the Last Five Years
23 New Federal and State Laws Resulting from the Women's Liberation Movement
24 The History of the "Initial Teaching Alphabet"
25 An Analysis of Attitudes Toward Slang Expressed by Linguists
26 Controls Used to Prevent Fraud in Scientific Experiments on Extrasensory Perception
27 An Analysis of Authenticated Cases of Faith Healing
28 The Consequences of Breaking Important Treaties with American Indian Tribes
29 Early Critical Reception of Plays in the "Theater of the Absurd"
30 The Origin of the Philosophy of Existentialism
31 A History of Changes of Rules in Basketball

12

32 The Reactions of Clergymen to Sinclair Lewis's *Elmer Gantry* (a satire on corruption in the clergy)
33 The Differences in Theological Beliefs Between Any Two Protestant Sects
34 Important Changes in Americans' Attitudes Toward Sex Between 1950 and 1970
35 Current Theories of the Origin of the Universe
36 Attacks by Scientists on Astrology in the Mid-1970s
37 Notable Thefts of Works of Art from Museums
38 Social Changes in the Chinese Community in San Francisco Within the Last Twenty-Five Years
39 The Feasibility of Urban Renewal
40 An Analysis of the Results of Important Teachers' Strikes in 1975
41 Women Governors: How Many Have There Been and How Did They Come to Office?
42 Important Retellings in English of the Arthurian Legends after Malory's *Morte D'Arthur*
43 The State of the Feminist Movement in the Early 1920s
44 Do Plants React to Music?
45 Mark Twain's Philosophy in His Old Age
46 The Reactions of Protestant Churches to the Supreme Court Ruling Barring Prayer in Public Schools
47 Jesus' Disciples in the 1970s: Who Were They?
48 The Journalistic Work of Norman Mailer
49 Sylvia Plath: The Last Year
50 The Kent State Killings: Was Justice Done?

Subject-Matter Areas for Research Papers

Many limited research-paper topics can be derived from the following fifty broad topics. If a particular subject-matter field interests you, go through the reducing process illustrated on pages 8–9 to arrive at a properly limited topic.

1 Pollution
2 Racism
3 Critical reception of various authors or books
4 The welfare system
5 Sex education
6 Political dissent
7 Transcendental meditation
8 Gun control
9 Space exploration
10 Parapsychology
11 Illegal drugs

12 Contemporary music
13 Art history
14 Basic beliefs of particular religions
15 Propaganda in twentieth-century literature
16 Consumer advocates
17 Prison reform
18 Effects of television
19 Advances in agricultural science
20 The Israeli-Arab conflict
21 The energy crisis
22 Educational innovations
23 Primitive religions
24 Behavioral and humanistic psychology
25 Radical organizations of the left or right
26 The American Indian
27 Occultism
28 Cancer
29 The history of the FBI and the CIA
30 Archeology
31 Youth and the social order
32 Afro-American studies
33 American folklore
34 Fashion
35 The news media
36 Women's liberation
37 Biography of famous individuals
38 Divorce
39 Astronomy
40 Language study or the English language
41 Political assassinations
42 Revival of old beliefs or customs
43 The cinema
44 Business and economics
45 Popular art or music
46 Crime
47 Pornography
48 Poverty
49 The vicissitudes of literary reputations
50 Political systems

Limited Topics for Critical Papers

The following fifty topics are sufficiently limited to be suitable critical-paper topics:

topics for research and critical papers

14

1 The Nature of Swift's Satire on Science in *Gulliver's Travels,* Part III
2 Aspects of Feminism in the Novels of Charlotte Brontë
3 Hemingway's Conception of the Nature of Love as Evidenced in *To Have and Have Not*
4 B. F. Skinner's Conception of the Perfectability of People as Expressed in *Walden II*
5 New York Society as Portrayed in.Edith Wharton's *The Age of Innocence*
6 The Importance of Peer Acceptance as Expressed in Theodore Rozak's *The Making of a Counter-Culture*
7 The Sardonic Wit and Common Sense of Dorothy Parker's Poetry
8 A Comparison of the Final Episode in Sir Thomas Malory's *Morte D'Arthur* with Alfred, Lord Tennyson's "Morte D'Arthur"
9 Characteristics of the Theater of the Absurd in Any Play by Berthold Brecht
10 Henrik Ibsen's Conception of Social Responsibility as Evidenced in *An Enemy of the People*
11 The Role of Chance in Thomas Hardy's *The Return of the Native*
12 Elements of Humor in George Bernard Shaw's *Anthony and Cleopatra*
13 Who Was Mrs. Rochester?: A Comparison of Jean Rhys's *Wide Sargasso Sea* and Charlotte Brontë's *Jane Eyre*
14 Satire on the Academic World in Bernard Malamud's *A New Life*
15 Absurdities in James Fenimore Cooper's *The Pathfinder*
16 Discrepancies in Psychological Theories in Eric Fromm's *Escape from Freedom*
17 Antiscientific Aspects of Pierre Teilhard de Chardin's *The Phenomenon of Man*
18 Career or Motherhood: Role-Conflict in the Poetry of Adrienne Rich
19 Rene Dubos's *So Human an Animal:* Religious or Humanistic?
20 Symbolism in John Steinbeck's *The Long Valley*
21 Contradictions in Germaine Greer's *The Female Eunuch*
22 The Fragmentation of Modern Society as Expressed in David Riesman's *The Lonely Crowd*
23 Dominant Themes in the Poetry Published in the *Atlantic* During the Last Fifteen Years
24 Elements of Satire in Joyce Carol Oates's *Expensive People*
25 The Different Views of the Nature of Evil as Expressed in the Book of Job
26 William Dean Howells's Conception of Realism as Expressed in *Criticism and Fiction*
27 Romantic Elements in Thomas Wolfe's *The Web and the Rock*
28 Humor as an Aspect of Jane Austen's *Emma*
29 Herman Melville's Religious Doubts as Revealed in *Moby Dick*
30 Nathaniel Hawthorne's *The Scarlet Letter:* Whose Was the Greatest Sin?

31 An Analysis of the Character of Flem Snopes in William Faulkner's **15**
The Hamlet
32 The Influence of Nature and Country Life on the Short Stories of Colette
33 T. S. Eliot's The Waste Land: Masterpiece or Hoax?
34 The Nature of Tom Paine's Religion as Expressed in The Age of
Reason
35 Allegory and Symbolism in Lewis Carroll's Alice in Wonderland
36 The Mississippi River as a Symbol in Mark Twain's Huckleberry Finn
37 Satire on Aristocratic Society in Henry James's The Americans
38 Autobiographical Elements in the Poetry of Dylan Thomas
39 Naturalistic Philosophy in William Somerset Maugham's Of Human
Bondage
40 Effects of Changing Social Patterns on the Characters of Ellen
Glascow's A Sheltered Life
41 Sir Toby Belch of Shakespeare's Twelfth Night: An Individual or a
Stereotype?
42 The Satiric Thrust of Voltaire's Candide
43 The "Black Humor" of William Burroughs
44 Sentimentalism in the Short Stories of Brett Harte
45 Regionalism in Sarah Orne Jewett's The Country of the Pointed Firs
46 The Nature of Human Alienation as Expressed in Peter Berger's The
Homeless Mind
47 The Theme of Death in the Poetry of Emily Dickinson Contrasted with
the Theme of Death in the Poetry of A. E. Housman
48 The Nature of Man as Expressed in the Poetry of Robinson Jeffers
49 A Comparison of the Heroines of Willa Cather's O Pioneers! and
Thomas Hardy's Tess of the D'Urbervilles
50 Propaganda in Upton Sinclair's The Jungle

Subject-Matter Areas for Critical Papers

Many limited critical-paper topics can be derived from any of the
following fifty broad topics:

1 Russian literature prior to 1917
2 Russian literature since 1917
3 The plays of Shakespeare
4 "Traditional" American poetry of the twentieth century
5 "Modern" American poetry of the twentieth century
6 English novels of the Victorian Period
7 Popular books on psychology
8 Popular books on sociology
9 The fiction of William Faulkner
10 Best-selling novels of the 1960s and 1970s

topics for research and critical papers

16
11 Novels of political protest
12 Novels of social protest
13 Biographies
14 Novels expounding the philosophy of existentialism
15 The theater of the absurd
16 The plays of Eugene O'Neill
17 The plays of T. S. Eliot
18 The poetry of Walt Whitman
19 The poetry of Emily Dickinson
20 The novels of Jane Austin, Charlotte Brontë, Albert Camus, Joyce Cary, Theodore Dreiser, Lawrence Durrell, Edna Ferber, F. Scott Fitzgerald, E. M. Forster, Elizabeth Gaskell, Graham Greene, Thomas Hardy, Ernest Hemingway, Henry James, James Joyce, D. H. Lawrence, Doris Lessing, Jack London, Bernard Malamud, Carson McCullers, Iris Murdock, Frank Norris, Anaïs Nin, George Orwell, Jean Rhys, John Steinbeck, Robert Penn Warren, Virginia Woolf, and so on.
21 The short stories of Sherwood Anderson, Elizabeth Bowen, Anton Chekov, Stephen Crane, F. Scott Fitzgerald, Nathaniel Hawthorne, Ernest Hemingway, O. Henry, Shirley Jackson, James Joyce, Franz Kafka, Katherine Mansfield, Guy de Maupassant, Joyce Carol Oates, Flannery O'Connor, Dorothy Parker, Edgar Allan Poe, Katherine Anne Porter, J. D. Salinger, John Steinbeck, John Updike, Robert Penn Warren, Eudora Welty, and so on.
22 The works of John Milton
23 The works of Mark Twain
24 The works of Colette
25 The works of John Keats
26 The works of Herman Melville
27 The works of Jonathan Swift
28 The works of Edith Wharton
29 French naturalistic fiction
30 Literature of the American Indian
31 Literature of Mexican-Americans
32 Black literature
33 Literature of Latin America
34 Literature of Nobel Prize winners
35 Regional or local literature
36 Detective fiction
37 Science fiction
38 A comparison of the styles of any two writers
39 The shift from formal to informal diction in American fiction
40 Pornographic elements in modern fiction
41 Political or religious propaganda in fiction
42 Books supporting women's liberation

43 Books attacking women's liberation **17**
44 Devotional poetry
45 The plays of Henrik Ibsen
46 The plays of George Bernard Shaw
47 Classical Greek literature
48 Classical Latin literature
49 Literature of the Renaissance
50 The works of any of the great philosophers

3
preliminary
reading and
outlining

PRELIMINARY READING

After you have settled on a limited term-paper topic, you should do a
small amount of work in preparation for using library source materials.
First, do a little preliminary reading on your topic, or on a broader topic
in which it is included, to be sure that you clearly understand what your
topic is and that you really want to write about it. For example, suppose
you start with the broad topic "Archaeology" and reduce it to the limited
topic "Important Archaeological Discoveries in the Bible Lands in the
1960s." Before using the information in Chapters 4 and 5 to compile a
full working bibliography, you should read an article or two pertaining to
your topic to verify your interest in it. You might, for instance, go to an

20 encyclopedia yearbook for the year 1965 and read its article on archaeology. Or you might look under the subject heading "Biblical Archaeology" in a library card catalogue and read a chapter in a recent book on the subject. Preliminary reading of this sort will either reassure you that you have the topic you want or will prompt you to seek another. In the latter case, your preliminary reading will have saved you needless work—it is discouraging to abandon a topic after you have spent a good deal of time on it.

When you do your preliminary reading, you should also ascertain whether sufficient source materials will be available to you. As you compile a working bibliography, you will discover the full extent of source materials available. But at this time you can quickly reassure yourself that sufficient materials are available by glancing at a subject heading in the card catalogue and one in the *Readers' Guide to Periodical Literature,* which you will find in the reference section of the library. For example, suppose you have started with the broad topic "Cosmology" and have reduced to the limited topic "Essential Features of the Theory of Continuous Creation." A quick examination of the subject heading "Cosmology" in the card catalogue and a similar examination of that subject heading in a recent volume of the *Readers' Guide* will probably assure you that you won't have trouble finding enough sources. On the other hand, if you have proceeded from the broad topic "Higher Education" to the limited topic "Ph.D. Programs in Russian Universities," a quick check of the card catalogue and of a volume of the *Readers' Guide* may convince you that so few sources are available that it is best to select a new topic rather than waste time on one that promises to lead nowhere.

PRELIMINARY OUTLINING

The better you understand your topic before you begin serious work, the easier it will be to follow the standardized procedures of compiling a working bibliography and of taking notes. As soon as you have done the preliminary reading described in the preceding section, you should try, as best you can, to come to an understanding of the main points your paper will develop. These points will form the first-level (Roman-numeral) outline headings of the formal outline you will probably be required to turn in with your paper. A formal outline is an aid for the reader and must adhere to a half-dozen principles of good outlining. A preliminary or scratch outline is for the writer and may take any form the writer finds usable. Thus in a preliminary outline, headings may take any form. An excellent way to approach your topic is to derive from it the few important questions your paper will answer. These questions will later be converted into outline headings, but they will serve as an excellent guide to your research and note-taking.

Suppose, for example, you have reduced and reduced the broad topic "Psychology" until you have the limited topic "The Use of Hypnotism as an Anesthetic." After some preliminary reading, you should ask yourself what important questions you expect your research paper to answer. Hard thinking might produce these questions: When, where, and how was it discovered that under hypnosis a person can be oblivious to pain? When and by whom was hypnotism first used systematically as an anesthetic? How have doctors and dentists used hypnotism as an anesthetic? What controversy has existed and does exist over the use of hypnotism as an anesthetic? What role do experts think hypnotic anesthesia will play in the future? Without such questions in mind, you will waste much time and will probably experience frustration in compiling a working bibliography and taking notes. With these questions before you, your work will be much easier—and undoubtedly your paper will be better organized.

Your preliminary outline will probably change and grow as your work progresses. You will update it periodically and add to it. For example, the question How have doctors used hypnotism as an anesthetic? might eventually produce these second-level outline headings:

A. Use in treatment of minor injuries
B. Use in minor surgery
C. Use in major surgery
D. Use in obstetrics
E. Use in cases of terminal cancer

Without the original general question (which would form a Roman-numeral outline heading), you might waste much time before conceiving the five clear subheadings just listed. Formulating the general questions makes deriving proper subheadings much easier.

Here are three additional examples of general questions that are in effect preliminary outlines. A preliminary outline would develop as the researcher's work progressed.

1. *topic:* Some Notorious Cases of Quackery in Cancer Cures
   questions: Why are cancer patients prone to being taken in by quacks?
   What have been the most notable cases of quackery and hoaxes in cancer cures since 1950?
   Have reputable medical doctors disagreed about supposed cures and if so, what was the nature of their controversy?
   What legal actions have been taken against quacks?

Is cancer-cure quackery diminishing and if so, why?

2. *topic:* The Growth of Abraham Lincoln's Religious Beliefs
   questions: What was the religion of Lincoln's parents, and what kind of religious training did they give him?
   What was his religious attitude as a young man?
   How did his religious views change as he grew older?
   Did he belong to a particular denomination and attend church regularly? If not, what seemed to be his definition of religion?
   Would his definition of religion be generally acceptable to church members?
   How did his speeches and writings reflect his religious sentiments?

3. *topic:* The Relationship Between Whites and Blacks in Mississippi in the Early 1900s as Evidenced in William Faulkner's *The Reivers*
   questions: How did whites demonstrate their belief in their superiority?
   How had blacks adjusted to the inequities of the social system?
   How much harmony existed between the races and how was it manifested?
   Did the system provide any special benefits for blacks?
   In what way, if any, did blacks express resentment of the system?
   Were there subtleties in the relationship between the two races that neither consciously understood?

Having such a set of questions or preliminary outline for your topic before you begin serious work on your paper will not only make your work much easier but will surely help you to write a better paper.

4
library
and other
source materials

After you have selected a limited topic, have done a little preliminary reading, and have prepared as much of a preliminary outline as you can, you are ready to compile a working bibliography. A working bibliography is a list of sources that will furnish information for your paper. But before you can compile a working bibliography, you must learn how to seek out and locate source materials in the library. This chapter is a guide to the research material available in most college libraries.

THE REFERENCE ROOM
AND THE REFERENCE LIBRARIAN

College libraries are complexly organized and function in different ways. Some allow students to go into the open shelves to select the books they

24 want. Others keep closed shelves and require students to present requests at the checkout desk and to wait for the books to be brought to them. Some libraries keep bound periodicals (magazines and journals) in a separate, closed room, and others allow students free access to bound periodicals either in the reference room or on other open shelves. Take care to learn how your library functions, in order to use it most efficiently.

Every library of even moderate size has a reference room open to all students. This room contains the reference works listed later in this chapter and sometimes contains the library's holdings in bound periodicals. To begin research for a term paper, a student usually starts in the reference room. Libraries of moderate size and larger always have a reference librarian in the reference room. One of the reference librarian's duties is to help those who have trouble finding what they want in the reference room. Don't ever wander around wondering what to do—go to the reference librarian with any problem connected with your research.

ENCYCLOPEDIAS AND REFERENCE WORKS

Most libraries keep hundreds of sets and single volumes of reference works in the reference room. Though you will not make extensive use of all of these works in preparing your term paper, a general understanding of them may prove valuable for future term papers.

The Limited Usefulness of Reference Works

Reference works are themselves compilations of research—covering thousands of topics in the case of general encyclopedias. An article in a reference work—for example, "The War of Jenkins' Ear" in the *Encyclopaedia Britannica* or "Kosher Foods" in the *Jewish Encyclopedia*—is not a suitable term-paper topic because complete research has already been done and published in one place. Remember that a topic is unsuitable if one source can supply all the information necessary for your research paper. Do not fall into the trap of thinking that you can change the wording of an encyclopedia article and have a satisfactory research paper.

In general, reference works have limited usefulness in preparing term papers, but you should by no means avoid them because they are compilations of research. Often an encyclopedia or reference-work article will provide good preliminary reading. For example, suppose you reduce the broad topic "Racism" to the limited topic "George Washington Carver's Views on Segregation." The biographical sketch of Carver

in the *Dictionary of American Biography* will not deal extensively with **25**
Carver's views on segregation, but as preliminary reading the article
will not only help you to decide whether you really have the topic you
want but will probably give you some information useful for your paper. Or, as another example, if your topic were "Jack London's *The Sea
Wolf* as a Naturalistic Novel," articles on naturalism and Jack London in
a general encyclopedia would provide you with sufficient preliminary
reading.

In addition to providing articles for preliminary reading, reference
works can provide useful information for many term-paper topics. Suppose your topic is "Some Baffling Accomplishments of Indian Fakirs."
Encyclopedia articles on "Parapsychology," "Psychokinesis," and "Psychic Phenomena" might contribute to your research, though they could
not supply enough material for your whole paper. Or suppose your topic
is "The Causes of the Strike by the United Farm Workers in California in
the Early 1970s." Since Cesar Chavez was leader of the strike, the article on him in *Current Biography* might provide some information for
your paper, though for the most part the article would be about aspects
of Chavez's life that would have little bearing on the causes of the strike.

General Encyclopedias

General encyclopedias have articles—in some cases very extensive
ones—on a great variety of topics. The following are the most important
general encyclopedias:

Chambers's Encyclopaedia, 15 vols.
Collier's Encyclopedia, 24 vols.
Columbia Encyclopedia
Encyclopedia Americana, 30 vols.
Encyclopaedia Britannica, 30 vols.

New editions of general encyclopedias usually appear about every ten
years, though most of them do publish yearbooks. These encyclopedias are as highly authoritative as general reference works can be.

Though some are more special than general, a list of yearbooks is
included in this section, for those put out by the general encyclopedias
are extensive, and the others are quite wide-ranging in their coverage.
Most contain articles on the extension of knowledge in the year preceding their date. For example, the *Statesman's Yearbook* for 1975 has an
article on political developments in China in 1974. A few, however,
such as *Collier's Yearbook,* cover the year given in their titles. Following
are the most important yearbooks:

The American Yearbook: A Record of Events and Progress,
    1911–1951

The Americana Annual: An Encyclopedia of Current Events,
    since 1923
The Annual Register: A Review of Public Events at Home and
    Abroad, since 1758
The Britannica Book of the Year, since 1938
Collier's Year Book, since 1939
Economic Almanac, since 1940
Facts on File: A Weekly Synopsis of World Events, since 1940
Information Please Almanac, since 1947
The New International Yearbook: A Compendium of the
    World's Progress, since 1907
The Statesman's Year-Book: Statistical and Historical Annual
    of the States of the World, since 1864
World Almanac and Book of Facts, since 1868
Yearbook of American Churches, since 1916
Yearbook of the United Nations, since 1947

Articles in yearbooks can be good preliminary reading for preparing a term paper. For example, suppose your topic is "The CIA's Illegal Tampering with the Mail from 1960 to 1975." The article on the CIA in one of the yearbooks covering 1975 would be a good choice for preliminary reading, for in that year Congress investigated the CIA extensively. Occasionally yearbooks can supply you with information usable in your research papers.

Special Encyclopedias and Reference Works

In addition to the general encyclopedias and yearbooks, moderately large libraries have from dozens to hundreds of special reference works, which are located on the open shelves in the reference room. Following is a list of some of the most important ones, grouped by subject-matter areas. In general, special reference works contain longer articles on any particular topic than do general encyclopedias. For example, the article on Jonathan Swift in the *Dictionary of National Biography* is much longer than the article on him in the *Encyclopedia Americana.* The general comments made in the preceding two sections apply to these special reference works as well.

All of these special reference works have editors or authors, but since the books are best located by titles, as are the general encyclopedias, the editors and authors are not listed here. Dates are listed only when they are pertinent. Supplements are listed. But you should remember that many of these works are periodically revised and that some may have supplements too recent to be listed here.

AGRICULTURE

Cyclopedia of American Agriculture, 4 vols.
Literature of Agricultural Research

ARCHITECTURE

A History of Architecture

ART

American Art Directory, cumulative vols. since 1952
Cyclopedia of Painters and Paintings, 4 vols.
Encyclopedia of World Art, 15 vols.
Harper's Encyclopedia of Art, 2 vols.
The Index of Twentieth Century Artists, 4 vols.
Lives of the Painters, 4 vols.
The Oxford History of English Art
Who's Who in American Art
Who's Who in Art (British)

BIOGRAPHY

American Men and Women of Science, 11 vols.
Appleton's Cyclopedia of American Biography, 7 vols. (Of
    famous Americans who died prior to 1900)
Contemporary Authors, 52 vols.
Current Biography, cumulative vols. since 1940
Dictionary of American Biography, 20 vols.
Dictionary of National Biography (British), 22 vols. and sup-
    plements
International Who's Who, since 1935
National Cyclopedia of American Biography, multi-volume
    set in progress
Who's Who (British), since 1849
Who's Who in America, since 1899
Who's Who of American Women, since 1958
World Biography, 2 vols.

BUSINESS

Economic Almanac, cumulative vols. since 1940
Encyclopedia of Banking and Finance
The Encyclopedia of Management
Encyclopedia of Accounting Systems, 5 vols.
Dictionary of Modern Economics

EDUCATION

A Cyclopedia of Education, 5 vols.
Education Abstracts, cumulative vols. since 1936

28

Education Index, monthly, with annual cumulations
Encyclopedia of Educational Research
Who's Who in American Education
World Survey of Education, 4 vols.
World Year Book of Education, cumulative vols. since 1932

HISTORY

Album of American History, 7 vols.
Cambridge Ancient History, 12 vols.
Cambridge Medieval History, 8 vols.
Cambridge Modern History, 13 vols.
Concise Dictionary of Ancient History
Dictionary of American History, 6 vols.
An Encyclopedia of World History: Ancient, Medieval, and Modern
Harper Encyclopedia of the Modern World: A Concise Reference History from 1760 to the Present

HOME ECONOMICS

Home Economics Research Report, cumulative vols. since 1957

LITERATURE

Cambridge History of American Literature, 4 vols.
Cambridge History of English Literature, 15 vols.
Cassell's Encyclopedia of World Literature, 2 vols.
History of the English Novel, 10 vols.
A History of English Poetry, 6 vols.
Library of Literary Criticism of English and American Authors, 8 vols.
A Library of Literary Criticism: Modern British Literature, 3 vols.
Mythology of All Races, 13 vols.
The Oxford Companion to American Literature
The Oxford Companion to Classical Literature
The Oxford Companion to English Literature
The Oxford History of English Literature, multi-volume set in progress

MUSIC

Dictionary of Musical Terms
Encyclopedia of Concert Music
Grove's Dictionary of Music and Musicians, 10 vols.
Harvard Dictionary of Music
The International Cyclopedia of Music and Musicians
Musician's Guide, 3 vols.
New Oxford History of Music, 10 vols.
Popular Music: An Annotated Index of American Popular

Songs, multi-volume set in progress **29**
The World's Encyclopedia of Recorded Music, 3 vols.
The World of Music, 4 vols.

PHILOSOPHY

*The Concise Encyclopedia of Western Philosophy and Philos-
ophers*
The Dictionary of Philosophy
Dictionary of Philosophy and Psychology, 3 vols.

POLITICAL SCIENCE

The American Political Dictionary
Cyclopedia of American Government, 3 vols.
Dictionary of American Politics
Dictionary of Political Science
An Encyclopedia of Modern World Politics
Palgrave's Dictionary of Political Science, 3 vols.

RELIGION

The Catholic Encyclopedia, 18 vols.
An Encyclopedia of Religion
Encyclopedia of Religion and Ethics, 13 vols.
The Interpreter's Bible, 12 vols.
The Interpreter's Dictionary of the Bible, 4 vols.
The Standard Jewish Encyclopedia
Twentieth-Century Encyclopedia of Religious Knowledge
Universal Jewish Encyclopedia, 10 vols.
Yearbook of American Churches, cumulative vols. since 1916

SCIENCE

Chambers's Technical Dictionary
The Encyclopedia of Biological Sciences
Encyclopedic Dictionary of Physics, 9 vols.
Engineering Encyclopedia
Handbook of Chemistry and Physics, cumulative vols. since
1913
The Harper Encyclopedia of Science
Hutchinson's Technical and Scientific Encyclopedia, 4 vols.
The International Dictionary of Applied Mathematics
The International Dictionary of Physics and Electronics
Mammals of the World, 3 vols.
McGraw-Hill Encyclopedia of Science and Technology, 15
vols.
Van Nostrand's Scientific Encyclopedia

SOCIAL SCIENCES

Chambers's Encyclopedia World Survey, cumulative vols.
since 1952

> *A Dictionary of the Social Sciences*
> *Encyclopedia of Psychology*
> *Encyclopedia of the Social Sciences*, 15 vols.
> *Encyclopedia of Social Work*, cumulative vols. since 1965
> *A History of American Life*, 12 vols.
> *The Worldmark Encyclopedia of the Nations*, 5 vols.

The reference room in a large library will have hundreds of reference works, but those listed above are sufficient for most term-paper work.

THE PERIODICAL INDEXES

In addition to reference works, the reference room contains a number of periodical indexes which record information on literature that is published at regular intervals: daily, weekly, biweekly, monthly, quarterly, and so on. Cumulative periodical indexes list articles published in hundreds of specified periodicals. These periodical indexes are especially valuable to students whose topics are concerned with contemporary issues because information on current topics is often found only in newspaper and magazine articles rather than in books or in reference works.

For students whose topics deal with nineteenth-century issues or events, there are two general indexes covering a wide range of magazines and a wide variety of subjects. *Poole's Index to Periodical Literature* will help you to find information dating from 1802 to 1906, while the *Nineteenth Century Readers' Guide to Periodical Literature* indexes the years 1890 to 1922.

A student preparing a term paper will probably find the *Readers' Guide to Periodical Literature* to be the most useful periodical index. The *Readers' Guide,* which begins at 1900, lists articles from about 200 widely circulated general magazines including once-popular but now defunct magazines, such as *Life* and *Look.* In 1953 the *Guide* began to index scientific periodicals. Every ten to twelve weeks a small volume of the *Guide* appears—only a few weeks lapse between the publication of an article and its listing in the *Guide.* The small volumes are combined until a volume covering two years has been compiled.

Articles are listed twice in the *Readers' Guide:* by author and by subject heading. Researchers seek out articles by subject heading much more often than by author. For example, if your topic were "New Developments in Energy Production," you would look under such subject headings as **SOLAR heating** and **GEOTHERMAL energy.**

The following is a sample of listings from the *Readers' Guide:*

WOLTERS, Richard
Pictures. il Writers Digest 56:6+ F '76
WOLVES
Showdown on the tundra. R. Rau. il Read Digest
108:147-50 F '76
WOLYNSKI, Mara
What men and women should know about each
other now. Mademoiselle 82:134+ F '76
WOMEN
Notes from abroad (cont) Ms 4:104-5+ F '76

Anatomy and physiology
See also
Menstruation

Crime
American women and crime. R. J. Simon. bibl
f il Ann Am Acad 423:31-46 Ja '76

Economic conditions
Displaced homemaker. A. McCarthy. Common-
weal 103:38+ Ja 16 '76

Employment
Job strategies '76. N. A. Comer. Mademoiselle
82:112-15 F '76
Women on the job. McCalls 103:68+ F '76
See also
Women—Occupations

Equal rights
Discreet victory; effects of wide-ranging laws
in Great Britain. il Time 107:49 F 2 '76
Due process and pregnancies. C. E. Polhemus.
Mo Labor R 99:64-5 Ja '76
Getting women off the boat and into the power
swim. M. Korda. Harp Baz 109:119+ F '76
Men and women together; legal aspects; adapta-
tion of address. R. C. Allen. il MH 59:21-5
Fall '75
Pregnancies and Title VII. C. E. Polhemus. Mo
Labor R 99:65 Ja '76
Second sex: 25 years later; interview; ed by
J. Gerassi. S. de Beauvoir. por Society 13:79-
85 Ja '76

Health and hygiene
Medical checklist for mothers. A. J. Goldberg.
Parents Mag 51:18+ F '76

History
Men & herstory. J. Jaffee; discussion. SLJ 22:
2 Ja '76
See also
Indians of South America—Women

Legal status, laws, etc.
See also
Women—Equal rights

Occupations
Emerging woman (cont) il Am Home 79:70-1+
Ja; 55+ F '76
Five women who began again. il pors Made-
moiselle 82:86+ F '76
Found women: Catron County, New Mexico. M.
J. L. Woodfin. il Ms 4:57-61 F '76
That career quandary. J. Marks. Seventeen 35:
25 F '76

As this sample listing shows, the authors' last names and the first word of a subject heading are in boldface capital letters. Some broad subject headings are divided into subheadings; for example, in the sample listing, the heading WOMEN is divided into the subheadings "Crime," "Economic Conditions," "Employment," and so on. If your topic dealt with an aspect of women and crime, the subject heading "Crime" would furnish you with a useful magazine article. The articles listed by author's name, such as WOLYNSKI, Mara in the sample above, are also listed under subject headings—WOMEN and men, as in the case of Wolynski's article. Often, of course, researchers must look

32   under a number of subject headings to find the articles they want.   For example, if your topic were "The Efficacy of Vitamin C in Treating Colds," you might look under the headings **VITAMINS, COLDS, ASCORBIC acid, PAULING, Linus,** and so on.

The title of each article listed in the *Readers' Guide* is given in full. The abbreviations that are used to list information about the magazine an article appears in are fully explained at the beginning of each volume of the *Guide*.   If such an abbreviation as Ann Am Acad is not immediately clear to you, you can look in the listing of abbreviations and learn that it stands for *Annals of the American Academy of Political and Social Science*.   The date of the issue of a magazine is abbreviated; for example, Ja '76 means January, 1976.   The volume number (if any) of the magazine and the pages on which the article appears are given as follows: 423:31–46.   423 is the volume number and 31–46 are the page numbers.   The symbol + following a page number means that the article is continued in the back of the magazine.   The abbreviation "il" means that the article is illustrated, and the abbreviation "por" means the article is illustrated with a portrait.   Other less commonly used abbreviations may be looked up in the front of each volume of the *Readers' Guide.*

Though the *Readers' Guide* may be the most useful periodical index for beginning researchers, there are many, more specialized indexes that students often find helpful.   They include the following:

Agriculture Index (includes books, pamphlets, and articles, from 1916)
Art Index (from 1929)
Biography Index (from 1946)
Biological and Agricultural Index (from 1964)
Book Review Digest (lists book reviews by author, title, and subject, from 1905)
Business Periodicals Index (from 1958)
The Catholic Periodical Index (from 1939)
Dramatic Index (American and English, from 1909)
Education Index (includes books, pamphlets, and articles, from 1929)
Engineering Index (from 1906)
Essay and General Literature Index (from 1900)
Index to Legal Periodicals (from 1926)
Industrial Arts Index (from 1913)
Poole's Index to Periodical Literature (covers American and English periodicals, most now defunct, from 1802 to 1906)
Public Affairs Information Service (covers books, pamphlets, and periodicals in economics, government, and public affairs, from 1915)
Quarterly Cumulative Index Medicus (covers medical literature, from 1927)

Social Sciences and Humanities Index (from 1907)
Technical Book Review Index (from 1935)
United States Government Publications (from 1895)

Most large libraries carry these indexes.

One other index—the *New York Times Index*—warrants special mention. Published monthly, with annual volumes since 1913, it indexes all important news stories, editorials, and feature articles that appear in the *New York Times* and gives not only the location of the article but a brief summary of it as well. Thus if you were writing a paper on an aspect of current foreign policy in the United States, you could find a number of articles about it in the *New York Times Index.* Even if your library does not preserve copies of the *New York Times* (many libraries keep the *New York Times* on microfilm) the *Index* may still be helpful, for other daily newspapers are likely to have published similar articles on the same day.

Cross References

Learning to use cross references in periodical indexes is an essential part of learning to do library research. A cross reference refers you to a subject heading closely related to the subject heading you are examining. For example, if you were writing a paper on some aspect of wine-making, you would look first for the subject heading **WINE-MAKING**. Some articles might be listed under that heading, and the phrase *"See also* oenology" might be listed. (Oenology means "the study of wines.") *See also* is a cross reference that sends you to a closely related subject heading that might furnish other usable research materials.

Cross references are especially helpful if you have a topic for which it is difficult to think of even one subject heading. For example, if you have chosen the topic "Methods of Teaching Reading to First-Graders," what subject heading would you look for? You might try both **TEACHING reading** and **READING** without success. But after more thought you might try **TEACHING methodology** and find not only that that heading is listed but that it has a number of cross references, some of which pertain to your topic. Skillful use of cross references will often reward you with a wealth of materials for your topic.

As the volumes of the *Guide* accumulate and grow large, cross references become more extensive. For example, in one four-week volume there were only three cross references for **LITERATURE**. But in a cumulative volume there were twenty-six cross references for **LITERATURE**, ranging from **AUTHORSHIP** to **SYMBOLISM in literature**. If your topic were on an aspect of literature, some of those twenty-six cross references would almost certainly provide you with useful articles. Though your topic might send you to the latest small volume of the

34 *Readers' Guide,* be sure to refer to one of the larger volumes as well because you will find the most cross references in one of the two-year volumes.

The Periodical Card File

An entry in a periodical index is useful to you, of course, only if the magazine containing the article you want is available. Most larger libraries have a periodical card file in the reference room, which will have a card specifying the available issues of each periodical in the library's holdings. Some smaller libraries enter periodical cards in the card catalogue, and others type lists of their periodical holdings. If, for example, a library did not subscribe to *The New Yorker* until the issue of July 11, 1932 (the magazine has been in existence since 1925), the card or list will indicate that the library has copies of *The New Yorker* dating only from July 11, 1932. The periodical cards and lists will also indicate any interruptions in the sequence of issues for any periodical.

THE CARD CATALOGUE

Although many term-paper topics send the researcher only to periodicals, others require research in books and pamphlets as well. The term-paper writer needs to understand the library's card catalogue. A library's card catalogue alphabetically lists all the books and pamphlets in the library's holdings (including the reference works in the reference room and occasionally including periodicals). Each entry is listed at least three times: (1) under the author's name; (2) under its title; and (3) under one or more subject headings.

Here is a reproduction of a card entered in the card catalogue under the author's name:

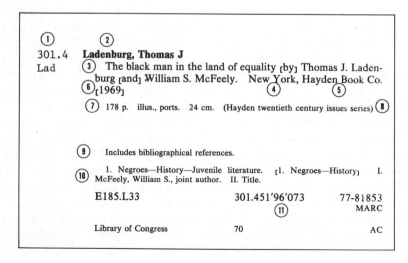

The encircled numbers do not appear on the card in its file. They correspond to the following explanations:

1 Call number
2 Author
3 Title
4 Place of publication
5 Publisher
6 Year of publication

7 Number of pages and size of book
8 A series the book belongs to
9 Bibliographical information
10 Subject headings
11 Information for librarians

Here is a reproduction of a card entered by title:

---

(1)   (2)
           The multicampus university
378.1   **Lee, Eugene C** ← (3)
Lee   The multicampus university; a study of academic governance,
        by Eugene C. Lee and Frank M. Bowen. With a commentary by
        William Friday.   New York, McGraw-Hill [1971]
     (7) xix, 481 p.   24 cm. $9.75   (5)   (6)
     (8) "A report prepared for the Carnegie Commission on Higher Education."
     (9) Bibliography: p. 469-475.

     (10) 1. Universities and colleges—Administration.   I. Bowen, Frank M., joint
      author. II. Carnegie Commission on Higher Education. III. Title.
      LB2341.L27   378.1   74-163849
      ISBN 0-07-010032-2   (11)   MARC

      Library of Congress   71[73]

---

1 Call number
2 Title
3 Author and co-author
4 Place of publication
5 Publisher
6 Year of publication

7 Number of pages and size of book
8 Comment by author
9 Bibliography of 6 pages
10 Subject headings
11 Information for librarians

And here is a reproduction of a card entered by subject heading:

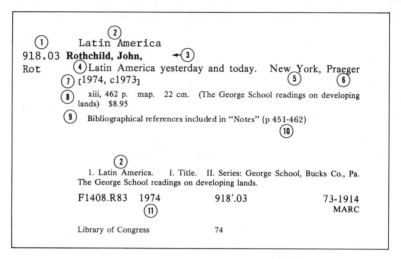

1 Call number
2 Subject heading
3 Author
4 Title
5 Place of publication
6 Publisher
7 Year of publication
8 Number of pages and size of book
9 Bibliographical information
10 Location of notes and bibliography
11 Information for librarians

Cross references are as important in the use of the card catalogue as they are in the use of periodical indexes. You will find cross-reference cards *after* all the cards listing the books under a particular subject heading; they fall under "see also." Here is a sample cross-reference card for the subject heading "Cosmology":

```
                    Cosmology

                    see also

        Astronomy
        Creation
        Earth
        Harmony of the spheres

        Philosophy

        Teleography
```

Sometimes only a few cross references will be listed for a particular sub- **37** ject heading, but in the case of a broad topic, such as "Political science," there may be a dozen or so cross-reference cards listing a hundred or more subject headings, from "Administrative law" to "World politics." When many cross references are listed, researchers must understand their topic well enough to select the cross references that are likely to be useful to them.

OTHER SOURCE MATERIALS

Though college students—and especially freshmen learning the process of writing term papers—do most of their research in the library, other helpful sources are sometimes available.

Personal Interviews and Documents

Occasionally a student may obtain useful information for a term paper by interviewing someone particularly knowledgeable about the topic. For example, in writing the research paper entitled "Therapeutic Uses of Music," which is reproduced in Chapter 10 (p. 103), the student interviewed a psychiatrist in a large county hospital. Another student writing a paper on "Moonshining" (producing illegal whiskey) actually sought out a moonshiner in the mountains of Tennessee and obtained firsthand information. Here are some other possibilities:

topic: "The Chief Causes of Divorce"
Interview a marriage counselor

topic: "Exploitation of 'Wetbacks' in Farm Labor in the Southwest"
Interview a farm-labor contractor

topic: "How Department Stores and Supermarkets Combat Shoplifting"
Interview the manager of a large store

Occasionally a student has access to personal documents that pertain to a term-paper topic. Say, for example, that a family has kept letters written by a relative who fought in the Civil War. If a student from such a family wrote on an aspect of the Civil War, the letters might yield useful information for the paper. Or, as another example, a family might have possession of diaries kept by a forebear who reached a high rank in politics. Such diaries might provide valuable information for a paper dealing with an aspect of politics or history. Such research

38   source materials are not often available, but they should be used whenever they exist.

Phonograph Records and Tapes

Increasingly, knowledge is being recorded on records and tapes, and such materials may, when applicable, be used in writing term papers. For example, a recording company produced a recording of George Frederick Handel's "Fireworks Music" that followed the original score exactly. Half of one side of the record was an explanation of how the recording was made. The original score called for an instrument called a calvary serpent, which the producers of the record had never heard of. But they not only found out what a calvary serpent is—a wind instrument made of leather—but acquired one. If you were writing a paper on "Some Long-Forgotten Musical Instruments," that record could provide you with useful information.

Tapes as well as records are used to record various kinds of information. For example, many of former President John Kennedy's speeches are recorded. If you were writing a paper on an aspect of the Kennedy administration you might well obtain usable information from them.

Films

Various kinds of films—chiefly documentaries—may also be used as sources for term papers. Many documentaries and nature films, as well as movies and television versions of stage plays, are now in the holdings of many colleges and universities, though usually in a building other than the library or in a separate wing of the library. If your library has a film that can furnish information for your topic, you should make use of it. Wherever your college's films are stored there will be a card catalogue listing them by subject heading as well as by title. You can search out films in the same way you search out books in the library.

5
the working
bibliography

Once you learn how to locate sources in the library, you are ready to compile a working bibliography. A bibliography, such as the one that will appear at the end of your finished paper, lists all the books, pamphlets, articles, and such sources as personal interviews, that have provided information for your paper. A working bibliography is a preliminary list of sources that you *hope* will supply the information you need to write your paper. Compiling a working bibliography before you begin to read and take notes allows you to examine sources in an orderly, productive manner. You will often be able to tell from your list of titles which articles or books to examine first. As your research progresses, you will find it necessary to revise your preliminary list of sources.

40   ENTERING INFORMATION ON BIBLIOGRAPHY CARDS

It is not necessary to check out a book or magazine in order to fill out a bibliography card. All needed information can be found in a periodical index, the card catalogue, or a reference work in the reference room. Standard procedure calls for listing bibliographic information on 3″ × 5″ cards. To avoid confusion, *never* enter more than one source on one card. When applicable, enter the following information on each bibliography card:

1 *The number of the card.* Cards should be numbered consecutively in the order in which you compile them. Numbering bibliography cards lets you conveniently identify the sources of notes on your note cards by a single number rather than by author, title, publisher, name of magazine, and so on—a procedure that saves much time.
2 *The library call number of a book or pamphlet.* If the book is one of a multivolume set, indicate either the number of volumes (for example, 3 vols.) or the number of the particular volume you will use. The library call number will permit you to check out the book without having to return to the card catalogue.
3 *The library call number of a volume of bound periodicals.* List the call number if your library does not keep bound periodicals on open shelves, or if your library shelves bound periodicals according to subject matter rather than by alphabetical order. Periodicals that are shelved openly and alphabetically generally will not have call numbers.
4 *The full name of the author.*
5 *The exact title of a book, pamphlet, or article.*
6 *The place of publication, the publisher, and the date of publication of a book or pamphlet.*
7 *The exact name of a periodical or magazine.*
8 *The date, volume number, and the inclusive page numbers of a magazine article.* In the *Readers' Guide* and other periodical indexes this information will appear in this form: "106: 16–17 Ag 11 '75," which translates into volume 106, pages 16–17, and the ussue of 11 August 1975.[1] You can either follow that form or alter it to suit your purposes; but you must record all of the information accurately. If the symbol +, meaning "continued in the back of the magazine," follows the page numbers in a periodical index, be sure to list that symbol on your bibliography card too.

[1] The British method of putting the day of the month before the month when the year is also given (11 August 1975) is used in footnotes and bibliographic entries in the *MLA Style Sheet,* which this text follows. You may wish to follow the same method in filling out your bibliography cards.

9 *For a newspaper article:* the author (if known), the title or headline, **41** the name of the newspaper, the city and state of the newspaper (if the name of the newspaper does not make them clear), the date of the issue, and the part (if any), page(s), and column(s) the article appears on.

10 *For a reference work:* the name and volume number, the title (and author, if known), and the inclusive page numbers. Also enter the library call number of a reference work so that you can find it easily in the reference room when you want to refer to it again.

11 *A note to yourself:* if the item has a bibliography of its own or some other special feature, such as illustrations, a note will remind you of its usefulness.

Here are some sample bibliography cards. The information on a bibliography card need not be presented in any particular pattern, since footnote and bibliographic forms differ considerably. You must be sure to enter complete information, however, and must be able to interpret it when you write your footnotes and formal bibliography.

```
                                                            1

    780.973
    H 83



        John Tasker Howard, A Short History

    of Music in America. New York, T. Y. Crowell

    Company, 1957.

            (Has ten-page bibliography)
```

card for a book

Card number 1 contains the library call number, author, title, place of publication, publisher, and date of publication—all the information you will need to check the book out and to write footnote and bibliographical entries. You know from the note at the bottom of the card that the book contains a bibliography that might suggest additional sources for your working bibliography.

> 2
>
> William F. Buckley, Jr., "Nixon's
> Pursuit of Peace," National Review,
> 1 August 1975, vol. 27, pp. 848-49.

card for a magazine article

> 3
>
> Robert Donovan, "Grade Inflation in
> the Universities," The Los Angeles Times,
> 24 June 1975, part IV, p. 6, cols. 1-3.

card for a newspaper article

Always recheck a bibliography card carefully to be sure you have included all needed information. When you are writing a footnote or an entry for the formal bibliography, it is frustrating to have to make an extra trip to the library to get a bit of bibliographic information, such as the date of a magazine article, when you could easily have entered that information when you wrote the bibliography card.

```
                                              4
R920.973
D 56



        "Lincoln, Abraham," Dictionary of

American Biography, vol. xi, New York,

Charles Scribner's Sons, 1933.  pp. 242-258.
```

card for a reference work

COMPILING THE WORKING BIBLIOGRAPHY

One of the first questions a student asks is "How many sources must I have?" Unfortunately, this question can't be answered precisely, for its answer depends a great deal on the term-paper topic. For a documented critical paper, a few secondary sources are usually adequate since most of the paper consists of a student's interpretation of some aspect of an author's work. For example, suppose you have chosen the topic "The Nature of Samoan Rituals as Described in Margaret Mead's *Coming of Age in Samoa.*" A half-dozen secondary sources would probably form an adequate bibliography. You could look under the subject heading **MEAD, Margaret** in the *Readers' Guide* for 1928–34 (*Coming of Age in Samoa* was published in 1928) and select five or six promising titles. Those, together with an early biographical article from a biographical reference work, would provide enough information for you to interpret Mead's description of Samoan rituals.

In research papers, the number of sources needed may vary widely. As a rule of thumb, a research paper for a freshman composition course should list at least ten sources that have actually provided useful information. A bibliography consisting of less than ten sources reveals that research has probably been inadequate. Some topics, however, are difficult to document. For example, with such a topic as "U.S. Business Investment in Iraq" you would probably feel lucky to find ten good sources. On the other hand, the topic "Varieties of Legal and Illegal Antiwar Demonstrations in the United States During the Vietnam War," might have so many sources that you would be faced

44   with the problem of selecting among them. For such a topic you would want to limit yourself to no more than forty sources. When compiling a bibliography, whether it lists ten or forty sources, be sure to include only those sources that have directly contributed to your paper.

Be methodical in compiling your working bibliography; don't wander aimlessly from one periodical index to the card catalogue, to another periodical index, then to the reference shelves, and so on. Where you start depends on your topic. Occasionally, with such a critical-paper topic as "Sinclair Lewis's Idealism as Evidenced in *Arrowsmith*," you should start with the card catalogue and will probably not need to go to the periodical indexes at all. You will want to find one or two biographies of Lewis and four or five books on the history of the American novel in the twentieth century. These books would provide sufficient secondary material for you to write your own interpretation of Lewis's idealism as revealed in *Arrowsmith.*

Normally, however, term-paper writers begin compiling their working bibliography in the reference room. Suppose, for example, you have chosen the topic "Literary Critic Edmund Wilson's Battle with the Internal Revenue Service." (Wilson, of substantial literary reputation, neglected to file income tax returns for several years.) To compile your working bibliography you should follow this procedure: first, do your preliminary reading in an article on Wilson in *Current Biography,* which among other things would tell you the year the IRS discovered Wilson's lapse of memory. (The year was 1961.) Fill out a bibliography card for the appropriate article in *Current Biography* and number that card 1. Next, see whether the *Americana Annual* or the *Britannica Book of the Year* for 1962 contain articles on Wilson and prepare bibliography cards if these sources provide useful information. Then go to the *Readers' Guide* for the years 1961–65, look under the subject heading **WILSON, Edmund** and make cards for any articles that seem promising.

Now you might consult the *Essay and General Literature Index,* the *Social Sciences and Humanities Index,* and the *New York Times Index* for the years 1961–62. Finally, go to the card catalogue. Look under "Wilson, Edmund" to see if a book title of his suggests that it discusses his problems with the IRS. (He did write a small book on this subject.) Then look under his name as a subject heading to see whether you can discover any books about Wilson that might discuss his tax difficulties. This procedure should uncover fifteen to twenty useful sources— quite sufficient for a research paper of 2000 to 3000 words. The main point here is that you should be thorough and methodical in compiling your working bibliography.

DECIDING WHICH SOURCES TO LIST

Often even a fairly large library will have only a small number of books pamphlets, and magazine articles that will yield useful information for some very limited term-paper topics. Suppose, for example, you have chosen the topic "Professions of Permanent or Semipermanent Black Residents in Switzerland from 1925 to 1975." Because of its location and unique history, Switzerland has not had large numbers of black residents, and thus not much has been written about them. Therefore in compiling a working bibliography for that topic you would be happy to find and list any books or articles about the history of blacks in Switzerland and would be content to find ten or twelve useful sources. Your task would be to *find* promising sources rather than to *choose* from among many listed books and articles the ones you think would be most useful to you.

More often, however, you will find in the periodical indexes and the card catalogue a large number of sources that seem likely to contain useful information. For example, suppose you have chosen the topic "Stirrings of Democracy in African Countries Between 1960 and 1970." There are many African countries and a great many aspects of their existence *besides* any stirrings of democracy that might have occurred in a decade. As you look under the subject headings "Africa," "African Politics," and the names of particular African countries, you will find listed hundreds of titles that were published after 1960. Most of the books and articles will not contain material pertaining to your particular topic. Even if they did, you could not examine all of them. What are you to do?

The answer is that you need to develop the ability to make a quick and accurate judgment as to whether a title is likely to be useful. For example, suppose in compiling a working bibliography for the above-mentioned topic you find the following list of ten titles under the subject heading **AFRICA** in a volume of the *Readers' Guide:*

1 "The First Elections in Nigeria"
2 "The Gentle General of the Congo"
3 "Immigrant Laborers in South Africa"
4 "Oil in West Africa"
5 "Political Debate in Kenya"
6 "Racism among African Tribes"
7 "The Russian Presence South of the Sahara"
8 "Safari into the Kalahari Desert"
9 "Starvation in Biafra"
10 "Uganda Expells Asians"

After some thought, you will see that numbers 1, 2, 5, and 7 might contain some usable information for your topic, but that the other six are unlikely to be relevant. You can't be absolutely certain they are inappropriate to your topic unless you read them, but in writing a term paper you are not expected to be exhaustive in your research. Thus it would be quite reasonable for you to quickly disregard the six unlikely articles and concentrate on those that seem most promising.

The better you understand your topic—that is, the better the preliminary outline you have made—the more quickly you will be able to
disregard unpromising sources and to enter into your working bibliography sources likely to be useful. For many, if not all, term-paper topics,
researchers need to be skillfully selective in choosing items for their
working bibliography.

CULLING THE WORKING BIBLIOGRAPHY

No matter how intelligently selective you are in compling your working bibliography, you are quite likely to list a few sources that are useless. You discover the uselessness of one of your bibliographic items,
of course, only after you have read at least a part of it. Students new
to term-paper writing often feel frustrated when they find they have
wasted perhaps a half-hour on a useless source. But it is in the nature
of research that a researcher tracks down false leads; this is an aspect of
term-paper writing you must come to understand and accept. In
Chapter 6 you will learn how to skim articles and chapters so that you
can either quickly reject the source or slow down and take notes.
        When you discover that an item on one of your working bibliography
cards is not useful, destroy the card. Do not worry about its number.
Gaps in the sequence of numbers on your bibliography cards are unim-
portant, for the number on a note card functions only to identify the
source of the notes.

ADDING TO THE WORKING BIBLIOGRAPHY

As stated earlier, your working bibliography is preliminary. Just as you
will sometimes find in it useless entries and will eliminate them, so,
after beginning reading and note-taking, you will occasionally be led to a
useful source that did not appear in your original working bibliography.
For example, suppose your topic were "Some Celebrated Cases of Censorship in Boston." You will undoubtedly read several articles men-
tioning the banning of James Joyce's *Ulysses* in Boston and in one of the
articles you might find a reference to the Boston censorship of the works
of Henry Miller. Perhaps, for some reason, you have neglected to include Miller in your working bibliography. You should now use this reference to lead you to more new sources. As your work progresses and
you discover additional sources, be prepared to add new cards to your
working bibliography.

6
note-taking

The previous five chapters discuss the preliminaries of term-paper writing. Though these chapters may seem packed with information, and the work they call for may seem formidable, you should be able to master that material with only a few hours of concentrated work. Now that you have a nearly complete working bibliography, your real work will begin, for note-taking and writing the paper are the two most important and time-consuming aspects of preparing a term paper. The work need not be tedious, and may well be enjoyable, if your topic interests you and if you follow the standard procedure carefully. This latter point cannot be over-emphasized. Most of the wasted time and unpleasant boredom that many students experience in writing term papers is due to their unwillingness to patiently follow standard procedures.

48   ARRANGING THE BIBLIOGRAPHY CARDS

After you have compiled your working bibliography (though you will continue to cull some items from it and add others to it), your next step is to arrange your bibliography cards in what you hope is the most productive order for investigating your sources. Just as you learned to be selective in choosing items for the working bibliography, you must also learn to be selective when choosing the best order in which to investigate them. You can't always be sure what the best order is, but you can learn to avoid thoughtless and random examination of sources for your note-taking.

Suppose you have chosen the topic "The Growth of Herman Melville's Literary Reputation from 1920 to 1950." Suppose too that your first four bibliography cards list these titles:

1 *A History of the American Novel,* 1921
2 *Nineteenth-Century American Fiction,* 1948
3 "The Whaleman of American Novelists," 1938
4 "Herman Melville: Neglected Genius," 1927

You might be tempted to investigate the items in chronological order, since you are to record the growth of Melville's reputation. Though that might be a workable order, it would probably not be the best order. For most topics, the best order for investigating sources is one that lets you read first the items that will provide the greatest amount of useful information. The reason for this is simple—you want to learn as much about your topic as quickly as you can so that you can make the best use of sources that might seem vague or irrelevant if read before you thoroughly understand the nature of your topic.

The best order for investigating the four items would be 2, 4, 3, and 1, even though item 1 is the first twentieth-century scholarly work to mention Melville. Item 2 is most likely to give you an overall view of how in a short time Melville emerged from obscurity to become one of America's most highly esteemed nineteenth-century fiction writers. With that overview, you are in a much better position to assemble pieces of information from other sources into a proper organizational pattern for your paper.

UPDATING THE PRELIMINARY OUTLINE

In Chapter 3 you learned how to prepare a preliminary outline for your topic, in the form of broad questions your paper will answer. Once you have arranged your bibliography cards, your next step is to update your preliminary outline as much as you can. For example, suppose you have chosen the topic "Controlling Fraud and Errors in Experiments in **49** Extrasensory Perception," and suppose that one of your broad questions is "How much fraud or error has been detected?" Among your bibliography cards are these three titles:

1 "ESP Experimenter Admits Transmitting Signals"
2 "Statistics in Rhine's Work Not Valid, Says Mathematician"
3 "Physicist Claims ESP Experimenters Allow Light Signals"

On the basis of these titles, you can update a part of your preliminary outline as follows:

> III. How much fraud or error has been detected?
>   A. Admissions of deceit by experimenters
>   B. Invalid statistical claims
>   C. Detection of fraud by impartial observers

The addition of the subheadings makes your note-taking easier because you know more precisely what information you are looking for.

After you begin to read source materials, you will update your preliminary outline whenever you can. The more quickly the organization of your paper develops in your mind, the more quickly you can take useful notes, and the better your paper will be.

SCANNING

As you have discovered, some items in your working bibliography contain no useful information and must be culled. You will also find that most items that do contain useful information will include much information that does not pertain to your limited topic. To save time and to avoid useless work you must develop the ability to scan, or skim, articles and chapters looking for words, phrases, or sentences that tell you you have found information pertinent to your topic. If you read slowly and plod through every item in your working bibliography, you will lose much time.

Having a good preliminary outline will aid you greatly in scanning. Suppose, for example, your topic is "Methods Now in Use to Prevent Extinction of Wild Species," and one of the questions in your preliminary outline is "Are there successful attempts to breed endangered wild species in captivity?" In scanning an article you will be alert to such words and phrases as "breed," "breeding wild animals," "births in zoos," and so on. You will pass your eyes very rapidly down a column of print, not absorbing what you read but looking for a clue that alerts you to infor-

50   mation useful to your paper. When you encounter such a clue, stop scanning and start reading carefully in order to take notes.

Here is an example to illustrate this procedure. The item from your working bibliography is entitled "Breeding Programs Aim to Keep This a Planet of the Apes." You have scanned the first page and found no word, phrase, or sentence that applies to any of the questions in your preliminary outline. But you persevere and continue scanning these paragraphs:

Stress on ape populations*

The yearly volume of trade in apes is not as high as the trade in most monkeys—fortunately so, for apes are much less numerous in the wild. Apes are also more expensive to obtain and maintain. Nonetheless, they continue to perish at a rate that wild populations cannot for long sustain. Both the Bornean and Sumatran orangutan populations, ostensibly protected by international agreements, remain under stress from poaching and smuggling, activities which persist mainly because markets exist abroad (See SMITHSONIAN, November 1973). A similar situation exists with lowland and mountain gorilla populations.

As it is such a popular subject in physiological, biochemical, immunological, pharmaceutical and other research oriented toward improving human health standards, the chimpanzee now heads the ape-import lists of many industrial nations. Several hundred chimpanzees are shipped out of Africa each year. The Asian gibbon, which is much smaller in size than the other apes, is just now becoming important in experimental research. The plight of the chimpanzee is immediate, that of the gibbon impending.

Clearly there is immense value in promoting research efforts that may uncover solutions to human illness and disease; it would indeed be presumptuous to ask that such research be eliminated simply because apes are vital substitutes for human beings in many experiments. Nonetheless, we would suggest that it is essential to know the full price being paid for these benefits by species other than our own. Benefit can only be measured against cost if both are known.

Many zoological parks and research institutions are trying to breed their nonhuman primates. All such efforts are commendable but, unfortunately, births are all too rare in these captive situations: Few zoos or laboratories manage to produce enough primates to satisfy even their own needs.

*From *The Smithsonian*, January 1975. © 1975 by The Smithsonian. Reprinted by permission.

Ape births are often highly publicized because apes are **51** exceptionally difficult to breed in captivity. A basic problem may be that captive apes are not really a breeding population at all, but a fragmented collection of individuals, pairs and small groups, of which many do not function as breeders. Rarely do zoos or laboratories have funds or facilities to breed their primates in social units which replicate or at least approximate wild breeding units.

When you get to the fourth paragraph and spot the phrases "zoological parks," "breed their nonhuman primates," and "births are all too rare," stop scanning immediately and begin careful reading so that you can take useful notes.

EVALUATING SOURCE MATERIALS

Some term-paper topics are purely factual and not subject to controversy. For example, if your topic is "Automated Procedures That Have Radically Changed the Printing Profession," you will simply search out the facts. With such a topic you will not be faced with evaluating your source materials—that is, passing judgment on their truthfulness and reliability.

Many term papers, however, deal with controversial topics, and where there is controversy you must learn to recognize biased, unsubstantiated material and to distinguish between facts and opinions. In writing a term paper you want to use only sound and valid sources, and that means you often need to evaluate your sources—not just to determine whether they pertain to your topic but whether they are reliable and objective.

Making sound evaluations of source materials is difficult, for many issues are very complex. But you can exercise a good deal of sound judgment, and you can learn to look for the kinds of clues that suggest that a piece of writing is not objective. For example, suppose your topic is "The Church as a Social Institution," and you encounter this passage at the beginning of an article entitled "The Purpose of Our Church":

There is an epidemic of dissent spreading throughout our fundamentally pure church. The religious spirit is unfortunately being replaced by a humanistic spirit, and autonomous groups, claiming to represent a purer Christianity, drift towards sociological and political views that are humanistic. These dissenters resist authority and try to gain devilish con-

trol over our church to make it humanistic rather than religious.

This passage is intended to sway emotions to an extreme, not to
examine an issue rationally and objectively. You should reject the article it came from as it presents unsubstantiated, biased opinions.

In evaluating source materials, you should take into consideration
(1) the reliability of the author, (2) the reliability of the magazine or the
publishing house; (3) the recency of the material if your topic is on a contemporary issue; (4) the completeness of the material; and (5) the distinction between verifiable facts and unproved opinions.

ASSIMILATING SOURCE MATERIALS

When you scan articles and chapters, you do not absorb all that you
read. As soon as your eyes have left a passage that promises no useful
information, you most likely will have forgotten what you read. But
when you are reading carefully and taking notes, you should assimilate
the essence of the information and make it a permanent part of your
mental storehouse. Don't just transfer information from source materials to note cards without letting it make an impression on your mind.
Remember, you are to become an expert on your particular topic, and
you should come to know more about it than what you put into your
paper.

NOTE-TAKING TECHNIQUES

Note-taking is essential to term-paper writing. Almost all students can
save time and effort by taking notes in a systematic way.

Orderly Preparation of Note Cards

Follow these directions for preparing note cards:

1 Use 4″ × 6″ cards.
2 If you write on both sides of a card, be sure to use a symbol to remind
you not to overlook any notes when writing your paper.
3 Never put notes from more than one source on one card.
4 Identify the source of the notes on each card by putting in the upper
right-hand corner the number of the bibliography card that lists the
source of the notes. This simple reference method saves tedious re-
copying of titles and authors and eliminates inaccuracies that re-
copying might introduce.

5 Be certain to include on each note card the exact page numbers from which you take your information. If notes on one card are taken from two or more pages of the source, indicate with a slash the point at which each new page begins. This will allow you to be accurate in listing page numbers in footnotes.

6 As soon as you have determined your first-level outline headings, put a Roman numeral in the upper left-hand corner of each card to indicate which part of your paper the notes on that card belong to. For example, suppose you are writing a critical paper on "Keats's Major Concerns as Expressed in His Letters," and the first two headings in your preliminary outline are:

> I. How much concern did Keats express about his health?
> II. How much concern did he express about his financial situation?

In taking notes you should put Roman numeral I on a card that discusses Keats's health and Roman numeral II on a card that deals with his worry over finances. You can even indicate second-level headings on your note cards. For example, the first Roman-numeral heading about Keats's health might have these subheadings:

> A. Distress caused by tuberculosis
> B. Concern about sexual adequacy

Enter I A on cards about his tuberculosis and I B on cards about his sexual worries. Indicating which part of your paper a particular note card pertains to will help you to arrange your note cards in proper order before you begin to write your paper—a method that will make writing the paper much easier.

7 Never put on one note card information that pertains to two or more different headings of your preliminary outline. Use only one card for each heading. A card containing information belonging to two parts of your paper would prevent you from putting the cards into the proper order for writing your paper.

8 Don't begin to write the paper until you have taken all your notes, but do update your preliminary outline when note-taking allows you to.

Summarized Notes

Except when you think you will use a passage or phrase as a direct quotation, take your notes in a condensed, summarized form. This will save time, since taking notes in complete sentences is time-consuming. You will expand the condensed notes later in your own words. Suppose, for example, your topic is "Rituals in Witch Doctoring," and one of your preliminary outline headings is "How do witch doctors behave when they

give treatments?" In an article by anthropologist Louis C. Whiton entitled "Under the Power of the Gran Gadu" you encounter this passage:

> Three of Raineh's assistants then attempted to lift him off the
> ground. He appeared to be in a tonic trance, his body rigid.
> Finally Raineh's assistants forced him to bend slightly at the
> waist. They supported him as he sat on the ground.
>
> A remarkable transformation then occurred in his facial
> expression and his personality. I recognized from my pre-
> vious experiences at such ceremonies that Raineh was now
> supposedly totally possessed by the witch and was no longer
> his usual self or in one of his priest roles. Raineh now became
> irascible and quarrelsome, and to everyone's surprise, he
> began to speak in English instead of his native *takki-takki*.
> Angrily he said, "I don't like these people" (the Bush Ne-
> groes) and, referring to me, "I don't like Lou," and other un-
> friendly statements. . . .
>
> The next step in the curing ritual was to transfer the spirit
> of the witch from Raineh to the altar of snake bones. I sat on
> the low stool and Raineh sat on the ground behind me, his
> shoulders pressed against my lower back. After a short time
> he began to utter what seemed to be undulating moans of
> pain, while the chorus continued to chant and shake the noisy
> maracas. Raineh proceeded to tremble violently, and when
> this ceased, his face gradually assumed an expression of gen-
> tleness and calm.

Your summarized, condensed notes might take this form:

Number 4 in the upper right-hand corner identifies the bibliography card that lists the source of the notes. Roman numeral II in the upper left-hand corner tells you that this information will go into the part of the paper covered by the second first-level outline heading. Pp. 22–23 tells you which pages of the article your notes were taken from, and the slash between "quarrelsome" and "Talks" shows that the notes before the slash are from page 22 and those after it are from page 23.

Note especially that some of the key words and some of the word order were changed in the process of note-taking. The purpose of this change (also one of the reasons for taking condensed notes) is to help to avoid plagiarism when expanding the notes to write the paper.

Verbatim Notes: Uses of Direct Quotation

Occasionally you will want to take verbatim (word for word) notes because you will probably use some direct quotations in your paper. In a term paper, a direct quotation may serve one of four purposes. First, a short direct quotation is often used to emphasize a point. For example, in a paper entitled "Controversy over Passive Euthanasia" you might have this sentence:

> Attitudes toward death have changed radically in the past century and we are, in the words of one author, "becoming less irrational than our forebears on the subject of euthanasia."

The quotation adds strength to an important point (of course the direct quotation would be footnoted).

A second use of direct quotation is to share with the reader a short passage that is striking and enjoyable in its phrasing. For example, in a paper entitled "The Public Attitude Toward Automobiles in the 1920's" you might have this concluding passage:

> In the 1920's a car was a symbol of joy and pleasure, not a symbol of power. As Lee Strout White said nostalgically about the Model T, "The days were golden, the nights dim and strange. I still recall with trembling those loud, nocturnal crises when you drew up to a signpost and raced the engine so the lights would be bright enough to read destinations by. I have never been really planetary [wandering] since. I suppose it's time to say goodbye. Farewell, my lovely."

This is an esthetic use of a direct quotation. You should not overuse direct quotations for these first two purposes.

A third and important use of direct quotation is to quote an authority to sanction a point of view that you support. For example, in a paper entitled "The Universe: Does Chance or Determinism Rule?" you might find this passage:

Heisenberg's Uncertainty Principle is by no means proven, and it may be replaced soon by new evidence supporting determinism. After all, Albert Einstein disagreed with Heisenberg, saying, "Der Herr Gott does not play dice with the universe." Einstein remained a determinist throughout his life.

Often, of course, longer passages of the exact words of an authority are used to give weight to a point of view.

The fourth, and also important, use of direct quotation is to present original evidence for a conclusion you draw. Suppose, for example, your topic is "Liberal Aspects of the Politics of Dwight Eisenhower." In reading his speeches and writings you might find passages that show that in some respects Eisenhower was liberal. You would quote parts of those passages as evidence for your conclusion.

In taking notes, be aware of the four uses of direct quotation so that you can take verbatim notes when you find a passage you want to quote. When taking verbatim notes be certain to (1) copy the *exact* words of the author and (2) indicate clearly with quotation marks what on your note card is direct quotation. Be sure to avoid filling your paper with random quotations. Use a direct quotation only when it fulfills one of the four purposes described above.

Plagiarism and Paraphrasing

One of the most deadly pitfalls in term-paper writing is plagiarism. Plagiarism is literary theft, or pretending that someone else's writing is your own. Since only a small percentage of your paper will consist of direct quotations, the majority must be your own writing. If you use the exact words of a source without putting the passage in quotation marks, you are guilty of plagiarism—and be sure to understand that simply footnoting such a passage does not remove it from the realm of plagiarism. If you use nearly the exact words of a source without crediting the author in a footnote or in the body of the text, you are also guilty of plagiarism. Taking summarized, paraphrased notes will help you to avoid plagiarism.

Paraphrasing means saying the same thing as the source but phrasing it in your own words. When you paraphrase you do not change the content of the information but you do change the wording and the sentence structure so that it conforms to your own style. Because you are compiling your information from written sources, you cannot avoid using some of the terms and phrases found in the original source. But you can vary your passage from the original by trying never to use more than five consecutive words of a source in any one of your sentences.

Here is an example of plagiarism in a research paper and an illustration of how the plagiarism might have been avoided. Notice that the

THE ORIGINAL SOURCE

The radicalism of Don Diego [father of the Mexican painter, Diego Rivera] became more and more unpopular with the authorities. He was publishing the weekly *El Democrata* to urge social redemption. He called on liberals to concern themselves with the poverty of the masses. When authorities became more displeased and when investments in some mines were lost, his wife persuaded him to move the family to Mexico City, a place toward which many were drifting at that time. His son did not want to move, for the climate was different, and he missed the beauty of Guanajuato. During the first year in Mexico City, the boy caught both scarlet fever and typhoid. When he was ill, his Aunt Vicenta taught him to read, and, young as he was, he read most of the books in his father's large library. When he was well enough, young Diego attended a drawing class at the Academy of San Carlos.

THE PASSAGE PLAGIARIZED

Don Diego's radicalism continued to become more unpopular with the authorities. He was publishing the weekly *El Democrata* to urge "social redemption." He called on liberals to concern themselves with the conditions of the poor. When he had had more and more trouble with the authorities and when his investments in some mines failed, his wife persuaded the family to move to Mexico City. This was a place toward which many others were drifting at that time. Little Diego did not want to move. The climate was different and he missed the beauty of Guanajuato. The first year they were in Mexico City he fell ill with both scarlet fever and typhoid. During this time, his Aunt Vicenta taught him to read, and he read through most of his father's library. As soon as he was well again, the boy began to go to a drawing class at the Academy of San Carlos.

THE PASSAGE PARAPHRASED

Diego Rivera, controversial Mexican painter whose work often bore a social message, was exposed to both art and to social problems at an early age. The origins of his social awareness may be traced to his youth, when the radical activities of his father, Don Diego, forced the family to move from the picturesque colonial city of Guanajuato to Mexico City. According to [the original source], it was the socialistic *El Democrata*, published by Rivera's father, that so enraged local officials. For Don Diego, the newspaper provided a means to advocate "social redemption" and to focus the attention of liberals on the "poverty of the masses."[1] The more Don Diego appealed to the liberal conscience, the angrier the authorities became. Yet the Rivera family did not escape hardship by going to Mexico City. As [the original source] states, the move almost took the life of the future artist, for he caught both scarlet and typhoid fever during the first year in his new home. When he re-covered, Rivera's father enrolled him in a drawing class at the Academy of San Carlos, and Rivera began his study of art.

[1]Use a footnote to acknowledge the source of direct quotations.

7
documentation

ABBREVIATIONS USED IN DOCUMENTATION

Here is a list of abbreviations you are likely to use or encounter in writing your paper.

A.D. "in the year of the Lord"; precedes numbers; no space between letters (**A.D. 640**)

anon. anonymous

art., arts. article(s)

B.C. "Before Christ"; follows numbers; no space between letters (**640 B.C.**)

c. *or* **ca.** *circa* "about"; used before an approximate date (**c. 1421**)

cf. *confer* "compare" one source with another; do not confuse **cf.** with "see"

ch., chs. *or* **chap., chaps.** chapter(s)

60

col., cols. column(s)

diss. dissertation

ed., eds. edition(s), editor(s), or edited by

e.g. *exempli gratia* "for example"; set off by commas (, **e.g.,**)

esp. especially (**pp. 210–14, esp. p. 212**)

et al. *et alii* "and others"; (**Charles Foreman et al.**)

f., ff. following page or pages (**pp. 6f.; pp. 90ff.**)

fn. footnote

ibid. *ibidem* "in the same place"; in the title immediately preceding (see pages 66–67)

i.e. *id est* "that is"; set off by commas (, **i.e.,**)

illus. illustration(s), illustrator, illustrated by

infra "below"; refers to portion of text that follows; "see below," however, is preferred

intro. *or* introd. introduction

1., 11. line(s)

MS, MS., MSS manuscript(s); use **MS.** when referring to a specific manuscript

n.d. no date

n., nn. note(s)

no., nos. number(s)

n.p. no place (of publication)

n. pag. no page number

n. pub. no publisher named

p., pp. page(s)

passim "here and there throughout the work"; (**pp. 10, 45, et passim**)

pseud. pseudonym

pt., pts. part(s)

rev. revision, review, revised (by), or reviewed (by); spell out "review" to avoid ambiguity

rpt. reprint, reprinted

sic "thus, so"; placed in brackets, **[sic]**, to indicate that a passage, especially one containing an error or some startling information, has been quoted accurately

supra "above"; refers to portion of preceding text; "see above," however, is preferred

trans. *or* tr. translation, translator, or translated (by)

vol., vols. volume(s); (**Vol. IV**)

PREPARING FOOTNOTES

Uses of Footnotes

In a term paper, a footnote may serve one of three purposes. One use of footnotes is to acknowledge the source of direct quotations. This type of footnote tells the reader the source and location of the quotation.

A second use of footnotes is to acknowledge the source of paraphrased information that the reader may question or may want to pursue further. For example, in a paper entitled "Notable Accomplishments of Nader's Raiders," you would footnote passages that detail specific accomplishments, such as forcing General Motors to recall automobiles with dangerous flaws.   You would not footnote such information as the name of Nader's lawyers, the lecture fees Nader receives, or the location of his headquarters.   A rule of thumb: *do not footnote facts that will pass without question.*   Footnote a passage if you think a reader might ask "How do I know that is true?"   It is not necessary to footnote paraphrased information that a critical reader will accept nor is it necessary to footnote simple and easily ascertainable facts, such as the birth and death dates of a famous person.   Many a term paper has opened with a sentence such as this:

> Ludwig van Beethoven was born in Bonn, Germany, in 1770.[1]
>
> ---
>
> [1] "Beethoven, Ludwig van," *World Biography,* 5th ed. (Bethpage, N.Y.: Institute for Research in Biography), I, 207.

Such unnecessary footnoting serves only to break the flow of the paper and to inconvenience the reader.

The third use of footnotes is to enter explanatory comments that would be out of place in the text of the paper.   For example, in a paper entitled "Critical Disagreement over the Quality of T. S. Eliot's Verse Plays" you might have this explanatory footnote:

> [3] An interesting sidelight: critics have been dogmatically partisan in their judgment of Eliot's poems.   Many maintain that the poems are of consummate quality while others label the poems obscurantist nonsense.

Explanatory footnotes, however, are seldom used in term papers.

Location of Footnotes

Some instructors prefer footnotes to be at the bottom of pages that have sources acknowledged, and some prefer all the footnotes to be on a separate page or pages at the end of the paper but before the formal bibliography.   The two sample term papers in Chapter 10 (p. 101) illustrate both methods.   You, of course, will follow your instructor's preference.

In entering footnotes in your paper, follow these instructions:

1 In the text of your paper, put a footnote number after the final quotation marks of a short quotation, at the end of an inset quotation, and at the end of a paraphrased passage of which you are acknowledging the source.
2 Use raised numbers, not numbers followed by periods, in both the text of your paper and with the footnotes themselves.

3 Number footnotes consecutively. This is necessary if they are together at the end of your paper, and it makes reference simpler if they are at the bottom of the page.

4 Indent each footnote as a paragraph. That is, indent the first line five spaces and put all other lines flush left with the text of the paper.

5 Single space each footnote, but double space between footnotes.

6 If your footnotes are at the bottom of the page, type a two- or three-inch line between the text and the footnotes. Leave a double space above and below the line.

7 In a footnote at the bottom of a page, omit the author's name if his or her full name has appeared in the footnoted passage.

8 If all footnotes are at the end of your paper, always use the author's name even if it has been used in the footnoted passage.

9 Be sure that your footnotes conform in punctuation and underlining to the forms illustrated on pages 63–66. You will probably find it more convenient to look at the required footnote form each time you write a footnote rather than to try to memorize all of the forms.

10 When you type footnotes at the bottom of a page, be sure to stop typing the text soon enough to leave adequate space for the footnotes as well as a one-inch margin at the bottom of the page. A guide sheet placed under the sheet of typing paper is very helpful in maintaining proper margins. The following illustration shows the bottom part of a guide sheet; the numbers are visible through most kinds of typing paper.

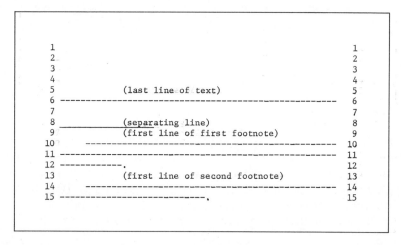

The numbers tell you how many lines are left before the one-inch margin at the bottom of the page. Be sure to allow for three lines between the end of the text and the beginning of the footnotes, between which there is a two- or three-inch line. If you see that you will have on one page two footnotes occupying a total of five lines, you should stop typing the text at number 6. Three of the remaining nine lines are for the spacing between the end of the text and the beginning of the footnotes. The two footnotes will occupy five lines, and the remaining line will accommodate the double spacing between the two footnotes.

Examine carefully the sample papers in Chapter 10 (p. 101) to be sure that you understand fully the ten points above.

Footnote Forms

The footnote forms below illustrate every kind of source material you are likely to use in preparing your term paper. These forms are modeled on *The MLA Style Sheet,* a publication of the Modern Language Association of America. Titles of articles, book chapters, short plays, and poems of less than book length are enclosed in quotation marks. Titles of books, pamphlets, book-length poems and plays, and names of magazines, journals, and newspapers are underlined. In these sample forms the underlining is continuous when the title consists of more than one word; your instructor may ask you to underline only the words and not the spaces between words. (The use of italics in the footnote forms below is equivalent to underlining in hand- or typewriting.)

Within the parentheses in these footnote forms are the place of publication, the publisher, and the date of publication. Note that a double space follows a colon but a single space follows all other marks of punctuation, except that no space is left inside parentheses.

A BOOK WITH ONE AUTHOR

[1] Janice Carroll, *Faulkner's Yoknapatawpha County* (New York: Random House, 1973), p. 82.

A BOOK WITH TWO AUTHORS

[2] John Herndon and Fern Jackson, *Mississippi Genius* (Bloomington, Ind.: Indiana University Press, 1969), pp. 21–22.

A BOOK WITH MORE THAN TWO AUTHORS

[3] Charles Foreman et al., *The New South* (Cambridge, Mass.: Winthrop Publishers, 1960), pp. 131–32.

AN EDITED COLLECTION OF ESSAYS, THE EDITOR BEING CITED

[4] Thomas Norman, ed., *Faulkner Criticism* (Oxford: Clarendon Press, 1975), p. vii.

64   AN EDITED COLLECTION OF ESSAYS, ONE OF THE
AUTHORS BEING CITED

[5] Joseph Micah, "Faulkner's Idiots," in *Faulkner Criticism,* ed. Thomas Norman (Oxford: Clarendon Press, 1975), p. 231.

AN EDITED WORK, THE ORIGINAL AUTHOR
BEING CITED

[6] William Faulkner, *The Sound and the Fury,* ed. Thomas Connolly (Chicago: The Wind Press, 1967), p. 103.

A WORK IN MORE THAN ONE VOLUME

[7] Pamela Stone, *Southern Fiction* (Atlanta: Southeastern Press, 1973), II, 142.
(**Note:** when both volume and page numbers are given, the abbreviations "vol." and "p." are not used.)

A TRANSLATED WORK

[8] J. C. Dougovich, *Faulkner's Universal Themes,* trans. Hugh Dick (New York: Harcourt Brace Jovanovich, 1975), p. 89.

A LATER OR REVISED EDITION

[9] Jesse Stone, *Faulkner in Virginia,* 2nd ed. (New York: The Viking Press, 1962), pp. 104–05.
(**Note:** if the book is revised but not given an edition number, then "rev." would replace "2nd.")

A SIGNED PAMPHLET

[10] John Logan, *Mississippi Freedom* (Jackson, Miss.: The Society for State's Rights, 1955), p. 10.

AN ANONYMOUS PAMPHLET

[11] *Commonsense Again* (Ackerman, Miss.: n. pub., 1956), p. 12.

A WORK IN A SERIES

[12] Lawrance Thompson, *William Faulkner: An Introduction and Interpretation,* American Authors and Critics Series, No. 14 (New York: Holt, Rinehart and Winston, 1967), pp. 55–56.

A CORPORATE AUTHOR

[13] President's Commission on Higher Education, *Education in the Humanities* (Washington, D.C.: GPO, 1967), p. 82.

AN ANONYMOUS BOOK OR PAMPHLET WITHOUT PUBLISHER, DATE, OR PAGINATION   **65**

[14] *An Illustrated History of Jefferson, Mississippi,* n.p., n. pub., n.d., n. pag.

AN ARTICLE IN A LEARNED JOURNAL

[15] Thomas Norman, "Darl's Madness," *College English,* 34 (April 1973), 920–21.
(**Note:** learned journals are defined as those paged continuously from issue to issue throughout a volume year. Their footnote forms are different from those of magazines that are paged by the issue. In the footnote above, 34 is the volume number. Note that the abbreviation "p." or "pp." is not used.)

AN ARTICLE IN A MONTHLY MAGAZINE

[16] Kay Jenkins, "Faulkner as a Farmer," *The Atlantic,* Sept. 1959, pp. 90–91.

AN ARTICLE IN A WEEKLY MAGAZINE

[17] Lucy Kowe, "Benjy and the Square," *Saturday Review,* 26 July 1969, p. 31.

AN UNSIGNED ARTICLE IN A WEEKLY MAGAZINE

[18] "Man Will Prevail," *Time,* 20 Dec. 1950, p. 48.

ARTICLES IN NEWSPAPERS

[19] Sally Owens, "The Friday Bookshelf," *Los Angeles Times,* 9 Dec. 1969, Sec. 4, p. 14, cols. 1–2.

[20] "William Faulkner Dies," *The Spokesman Review* (Spokane, Wash.), 22 July 1962, p. 1, cols. 5–6.

ARTICLES IN REFERENCE WORKS

[21] J[ames] E[lliott] W[almsley], "Faulkner, Charles James," *Dictionary of American Biography* (New York: Charles Scribner's Sons, 1931), VI, 298.
(**Note:** articles in many reference works are signed with initials. The author's full name is listed in the index volume. The part of the name not given with the initials is put in brackets in the footnote. Some reference works do not list the authors of the various articles:
[22] "Faulkner, William," *Current Biography 1951* (New York: H. W. Wilson Company, 1952), p. 192.

66   A PERSONAL INTERVIEW

[23] Interview with John Colby, Professor of English, Univ. of Miss., Oxford, Miss., 10 July 1975.

A PERSONAL DOCUMENT

[24] Deborah Faulkner, unpublished diary, entry for 6 Jan. 1903.

A LECTURE

[25] Leon Howard, "Faulkner's Humor," lecture presented at the Univ. of New Mexico, 10 March 1975.

A RECORDING OR TAPE

[26] A. H. Wilson, "Readings from Faulkner's Fiction, with Commentary" (New York: Westminster Company), recording No. PL 4025, side 2.

A TELEVISION PROGRAM

[27] "William Faulkner," in *Great Men Series*, narrated by Joseph Fletcher (New York: NBC–TV 6 March 1975).

A FILM

[28] *A Tour of Faulkner Country*, film narrated by James Elliott (New York: Documentary Films, 1971).

Subsequent References

Once a source has been footnoted, subsequent references to it may be a short form. If a reference is identical to the reference immediately preceding except for page number, the abbreviation ibid., meaning "in the same place," should be used. It should not be underlined (italicized) but should be capitalized. If the page number is the same, ibid. alone will suffice.

[29] John Faulkner, *My Brother Bill* (New York: Norton, 1963), p. 18.
[30] Ibid.
[31] Ibid., p. 29.

If an author has only one work cited, just the last name and the page number make a short form. If two authors with the same last name have been cited, the full name is needed in a short form. If an author has more than one work cited, the short form must be the last **67** name of the author, the title (shortened, if convenient), and the page number. The short form for an anonymous work consists of the title and page number.

> [32] Carroll, p. 82.
> [33] Pamela Stone, p. 142.
> [34] Norman, "Darl's Madness," p. 923.
> [35] "Man Will Prevail," p. 48.

PREPARING THE BIBLIOGRAPHY

At the end of your paper you will present a formal bibliography of the sources you have used. The following list will help you to prepare your formal bibliography:

1 List all sources you used to write your paper, including those for which no footnote entries were made. Do not list sources that were of no use to you.
2 Start the bibliography on a new page, regardless of how much blank space may be left on the final page of text.
3 Type the heading Bibliography centered one and one-quarter inches from the top of the page.
4 List all bibliographic entries alphabetically.
5 Enter anonymous titles by the first word of the title (except for *a, an,* and *the*).
6 Put the author's last name first. In the case of a book with two authors, the name of the second author retains its normal order.
7 With more than two authors, use the name of the first author in conjunction with "et al."
8 If you list two or more entries for the same author, substitute a long dash (_____.) for his or her name after its first use. Use secondary alphabetizing by first word of title (except for *a, an,* and *the*).
9 Have the first line of a bibliographic entry flush left, with a one and one-quarter-inch margin. Indent all subsequent lines five spaces.
10 Do not number bibliographic entries.
11 Single space each entry, but double space between entries.

Study the formal bibliographies at the end of each sample paper in Chapter 10 (p. 101) to be sure that you understand the procedures discussed above.

Bibliography Forms

The bibliographic forms below illustrate all the sources you are likely to use in term-paper writing. These forms are modeled on *The MLA Style Sheet*. As with footnote forms, you will probably find it more convenient to refer to the required bibliographic form each time you write an entry rather than to try to memorize all the forms. See page 63 for instructions about underlining and about indicating titles of long and short works.

A BOOK WITH ONE AUTHOR

Carroll, Janice. *Faulkner's Yoknapatawpha County*. New York: Random House, 1973.

A BOOK WITH TWO AUTHORS

Herndon, John, and Fern Jackson. *Mississippi Genius*. Bloomington, Ind.: Indiana University Press, 1969.

A BOOK WITH MORE THAN TWO AUTHORS

Foreman, Charles, et al. *The New South*. Cambridge, Mass.: Winthrop Publishers, 1960.

AN EDITED COLLECTION OF ESSAYS

Faulkner Criticism. Ed. Thomas Norman. Oxford: Clarendon Press, 1975.

A COMPONENT PART OF A BOOK

Micah, Joseph. "Faulkner's Idiots." *Faulkner Criticism*. Ed. Thomas Norman. Oxford: Clarendon Press, 1975. Pp. 230–38.

AN EDITED WORK

Faulkner, William. *The Sound and the Fury*. Ed. Thomas Connolly. Chicago: The Wind Press, 1967.

A WORK IN MORE THAN ONE VOLUME

Stone, Pamela. *Southern Fiction*. 2 vols. Atlanta: Southeastern Press, 1973.

A TRANSLATED WORK

Dougovich, J. C. *Faulkner's Universal Themes*. Trans. Hugh Dick. New York: Harcourt Brace Jovanovich, 1975.

A LATER OR REVISED EDITION

Stone, Jesse. *Faulkner in Virginia.* 2nd ed. New York: The Viking Press, 1962.
(**Note:** if the book is revised but has no edition number, "rev." would replace "2nd.")

A SIGNED PAMPHLET

Logan, John. *Mississippi Freedom.* Jackson, Miss.: The Society for State's Rights, 1955.

AN ANONYMOUS PAMPHLET

Commonsense Again. Ackerman, Miss.: n. pub., 1956.

A WORK IN A SERIES

Thompson, Lawrance. *William Faulkner: An Introduction and Interpretation.* American Authors and Critics Series, No. 14. New York: Holt, Rinehart and Winston, 1967.

A CORPORATE AUTHOR

Education in the Humanities. President's Commission of Higher Education. Washington, D.C.: GPO, 1967.

AN ANONYMOUS BOOK OR PAMPHLET WITHOUT PUBLISHER OR DATE

An Illustrated History of Jefferson, Mississippi. N.p., n. pub., n.d.

AN ARTICLE IN A LEARNED JOURNAL

Norman, Thomas. "Darl's Madness." *College English,* 34 (April 1973), 920–25.
(**Note:** 34 is the volume number. The abbreviation pp. is not used in this form. See note accompanying footnote 15 on page 65.)

AN ARTICLE IN A MONTHLY MAGAZINE

Jenkins, Kay. "Faulkner as a Farmer." *The Atlantic,* Sept. 1959, pp. 90–91 ff.
(**Note:** ff. tells the reader that the article goes beyond page 91 but that there are intervening pages, usually of other articles and advertisements.)

AN ARTICLE IN A WEEKLY MAGAZINE

Kowe, Lucy. "Benjy and the Square." *Saturday Review,* 26 July 1969, pp. 30–32.

70 AN UNSIGNED ARTICLE IN A WEEKLY MAGAZINE

"Man Will Prevail." *Time,* 20 Dec. 1950, pp. 48–49.

ARTICLES IN NEWSPAPERS

Owens, Sally. "The Friday Bookshelf." *Los Angeles Times,* 9 Dec. 1969, Sec. 4, p. 14, cols. 1–2.
"William Faulkner Dies." *The Spokesman Review* (Spokane, Wash.), 22 July 1962, p. 1, cols. 5–6.

ARTICLES IN REFERENCE WORKS

W[almsley], J[ames] E[lliott]. "Faulkner, Charles James." *Dictionary of American Biography.* New York: Charles Scribner's Sons, 1931. VI, 298–99.
(**Note:** see note accompanying footnote 21 on page 65.)
"Faulkner, William." *Current Biography 1951.* New York: H. W. Wilson Company, 1952. Pp. 192–94.

A PERSONAL INTERVIEW

Interview with John Colby, Professor of English, Univ. of Miss. Oxford, Miss., 10 July 1975.

A PERSONAL DOCUMENT

Faulkner, Deborah. Unpublished diary for the years 1902–04.

A LECTURE

Howard, Leon. "Faulkner's Humor." Lecture presented at the Univ. of New Mexico, 10 March 1975.

A RECORDING OR TAPE

Wilson, A. H. "Readings from Faulkner's Fiction, with Commentary." Westminster Company recording, No. PL 4025.

A TELEVISION PROGRAM

"William Faulkner." *Great Men Series.* Narrated by Joseph Fletcher. New York: NBC–TV, 6 March 1975.

A FILM

A Tour of Faulkner Country. Film narrated by James Elliott. New York: Documentary Films, 1971.

8
the formal
outline

The preliminary outline is for the writer's use and need not observe all the principles of formal outlining. The formal outline is for the reader. Your instructor may ask you to submit a formal outline with your paper. Although you can wait until you have written your paper to prepare the formal outline, transforming your preliminary outline into a formal outline *before* you begin your paper may make the writing easier, since the organization of your paper will be more firmly impressed on your mind. Therefore, this chapter on the formal outline precedes the chapter on writing the paper.

Even though you will probably have a separate title page, the title of your paper should be centered at the top of your outline page, with a one and one-quarter-inch margin. The heading **Outline** should be centered under the title. Many, if not most, instructors also like a thesis sentence, which states the central idea of the paper, to precede the first heading of the outline. Examine the sample papers in Chapter 10 (p. 101) for illustrations of these points.

TOPIC AND SENTENCE OUTLINES

An outline may be either a topic outline or a sentence outline. The two types are distinguished by the grammatical construction of the headings. A topic outline has phrases or dependent clauses as headings; a sentence outline has complete sentences as headings. Never use both kinds in one outline. You, of course, will follow your instructor's preference in choosing between the two kinds of outlines. Throughout this chapter, however, points will be illustrated with topic headings, for they can be easily transformed into sentences. Here is an example of the two kinds of outline:

topic outline: I. Faulkner's literary efforts at the University of Mississippi
  A. His work on the university literary magazine
  B. His first attempts at the university at writing short stories
sentence outline: I. Faulkner engaged in literary efforts at the University of Mississippi.
  A. He worked on the university literary magazine.
  B. He made his first attempts at the university at writing short stories.

CONSISTENCY OF FORM

Most outlines follow this numbering system:

  I. First level
    A. Second level
      1. Third level
        a. Fourth level
          (1). Fifth level

Writers of topic outlines do not generally put periods at the end of their headings. Whatever system you use, be consistent.

The purpose of a formal outline is to give the reader a quick understanding of the main points of the paper and of the order of their development. An outline heading is, in a sense, the title of a part of the paper; that is, a capsule summary of one or more paragraphs. To be properly balanced, an outline should have as many headings as a paper has general points. If an outline has too few headings, the reader will not learn much from it. If it has too many headings, some will state specific rather than general points, and the reader will, in effect, be given the entire paper rather than a capsule summary. A rule of thumb: never use an outline heading that covers only one sentence in the paper. Seldom should an outline for a paper of 2000 to 3000 words have more than three levels; quite often a two-level outline is sufficient. Remember that a formal outline is a summary of general points, not a restatement of the whole paper.

Here is an example of an improperly balanced outline that has too few headings:

THE RELIGIOUS VIEWS OF ABRAHAM LINCOLN

   I. The controversy over Lincoln's religious views
  II. His early contact with fundamentalist religious concepts
 III. His religious skepticism in early adulthood
 IV. His religious development in Springfield
  V. His further religious development as president

This is a good outline as far as it goes, but it is too scant. It needs subheadings to provide the reader with a fuller understanding of the first-level headings.

Here is an example of part of an improperly balanced outline that has too many headings:

THE RELIGIOUS VIEWS OF ABRAHAM LINCOLN

I. The controversy over Lincoln's religious views
  A. William Herndon's portrayal of Lincoln as a nonbeliever
    1. Herndon's religious zeal
      a. His constant proselytizing
      b. His anger when rebuffed
    2. Herndon's dislike of Lincoln
      a. Felt Lincoln scorned him
      b. Determined to get revenge
        (1) Took every opportunity to slander Lincoln
        (2) Tried to goad Lincoln into counterattack
  B. Claims by ministers that Lincoln was an orthodox Christian

74   This is a poor outline because it goes into too much detail. Some of the fourth- and fifth-level headings would cover only one or two sentences of the paper.

Here is an example of part of an outline that is properly balanced:

THE RELIGIOUS VIEWS OF ABRAHAM LINCOLN

I. The controversy over Lincoln's religious views
   A. William Herndon's portrayal of Lincoln as a nonbeliever
   B. Claims by ministers that Lincoln was an orthodox Christian
   C. Conflicting evidence in the arguments of both sides
   D. A resolution of the controversy
      1. The complex nature of Lincoln's religion
      2. The gradual development of his religious views

An outline as properly balanced as the segment above furnishes readers with a general understanding of the organization and main points of the paper but does not tell them everything the paper has to say. A term-paper outline should have at least two levels, but no more than three. This rule, however, does *not* apply to each first-level (Roman-numeral) heading. A good outline might be comprised of one or more first-level headings with no subheadings, one or more first-level headings with second-level subheadings only, and one or more first-level headings with second- and third-level subheadings. The number of headings and subheadings in the outline depends on how many general points the paper develops.

MEANINGFUL HEADINGS

A formal outline is worthless if its headings are so vague that readers learn little from them. The headings of a good outline should be meaningful to those who have not read the paper, for the purpose of the formal outline is to give readers a quick overview of the paper before they read it. For that reason, never use *introduction* and *conclusion* as outline headings. All readers will know that the paper begins and ends.

Here is an example of near-meaningless headings:

DOMINANT THEMES IN THE SHORT POEMS OF ROBINSON JEFFERS

I. Humanity and nature
II. Civilization
III. Nature

Such headings tell the reader little, if anything, about the content of the **75**
paper. The headings can be made meaningful by adding information:

    I. Jeffers's view of what humanity's relationship to nature
      should be
   II. Jeffers's rejection of human civilization as a standard for
      judging the meaning of life
  III. Jeffers's acceptance of "nature red in tooth and claw" as
      the universal law of nature

Now the reader has a good preview of the paper, for the outline headings
are informative and meaningful. (A full outline for this topic would be
more extensive than this example.)

PARALLELISM OF CONTENT

An outline is composed of levels, and the headings in any one level are
divisions of the preceding higher level. The first-level (Roman-numeral)
headings are divisions of the title. An outline should be constructed so
that all the headings on any one level are parallel or equal to each other
in content.
    Here is an example of faulty parallelism of content:

THE EFFICACY OF NONVIOLENT RESISTANCE IN ACHIEVING CIVIL RIGHTS

    I. Its success in giving law-enforcement agencies a bad
      public image
   II. Through exposing the existence of some police brutality
  III. Through making the law-enforcement agencies appear to
      be the aggressors

The parallelism of content is faulty in this example because Roman numerals II and III are divisions of Roman numeral I, not of the title. They
should be second-level headings (A and B) under Roman numeral I.
    Here is another example of faulty parallelism of content:

THOREAU'S REJECTION OF THE PROTESTANT ETHIC AS EVIDENCED IN *WALDEN*

  I. Thoreau's attitude toward amassment of wealth
    A. His refusal to acknowledge work as a duty
    B. His rejection of a Christian fundamentalism

Parallelism of content in this segment of an outline is faulty because

76   headings A and B are not divisions of Roman numeral I but of the title. They should be Roman numerals II and III.

Parallelism of content requires headings on any one level to be equal to each other in the kind of meaning they convey. This does not mean, however, that the amount of space devoted to, say, second-level headings must be consistent throughout the paper; that is, it would be quite acceptable for heading I.A. to summarize the content of a full page while heading I.B. summarizes less than half a page. Subheadings A and B must be divisions of Roman numeral I in the kind of meaning they express, not in the amount of space each occupies in the paper.

PARALLELISM OF STRUCTURE

As you have learned, outlines are composed of levels, with Roman-numeral headings being level one, capital-letter headings level two, Arabic-numeral headings level three, and so on. But outlines are also composed of divisions. All the Roman-numeral headings, being divisions of the title, are one division. All the capital-letter headings under any one Roman-numeral heading, being divisions of that heading, are one division. All the Arabic-numeral headings under any one capital-letter heading, being divisions of that heading, are also one division. But the capital-letter headings under a particular Roman-numeral heading are a different division from the capital-letter headings under another Roman-numeral heading, and so on.

The principle of parallelism of structure in outlining is that the headings in any *one* division must have the same grammatical structure. For example, if Roman numeral I is a noun phrase (such as "The uses of bear grease"), all the remaining Roman-numeral headings, all being divisions of the title, must be noun phrases (or at least nominals of some sort). Similarly, if heading A under Roman numeral I is an infinitive phrase (such as "To prevent baldness"), all other capital-letter headings under Roman numeral I, being in one division, must be infinitive phrases. Capital-letter headings under Roman numeral II in the same outline would not have to be infinitive phrases, since they fall under a different division. The principle of parallelism of structure is that all headings in any *one* division must be in the same grammatical structure.

Here is an example of faulty parallelism of structure:

THE CURRENT CONTROVERSY OVER
THE VALIDITY OF ASTROLOGY

I. The views of professional astronomers on astrology

A. Their insistence that no valid experiments support astrology **77**

B. Maintaining that stars are too far away to influence life on earth

C. In agreement with other scientists that astrology is a fraud

II. Most clergymen oppose astrology.

Roman numerals I and II are not parallel in structure, for I is a noun phrase and II is a complete sentence. Similarly, the three capital-letter headings under I are not parallel: A is a noun phrase; B is a present-participial phrase; and C is a prepositional phrase.

Here is the same portion of the outline with parallel grammatical structures:

I. The views of professional astronomers on astrology

A. Their insistence that no valid experiments support astrology

B. Their claim that the stars are too far away to influence life on earth

C. Their agreement with other scientists that astrology is fraudulent

II. The views of clergymen on astrology

Now the headings in each of these two divisions are parallel in structure. I and II are both noun phrases, and A, B, and C are also all noun phrases. Although noun phrases are the most common grammatical structure in topic outlines, dependent clauses and other kinds of phrases often make good topic headings.

USE OF SINGLE SUBHEADINGS

Since outlining is a matter of dividing general headings into less general headings, single subheadings usually represent a flaw in outlining (when anything is divided it must be divided into at least two parts). Here is an example of faulty use of single subheadings:

METHODS OF COPING WITH HYPERKINETIC
CHILDREN

I. Ways to reduce the excessive activity of hyperkinetic children

A. The use of certain antidepressant drugs

B. The use of attention-getting devices

C. The development of responsibility factors

1. Giving the child responsibilities in the classroom

78   First, Roman numeral I is a faulty single subheading, for it is just a restatement of the title, not a division of the title. Roman numeral I should be deleted, and A, B, and C should become I, II, and III. Second, the heading 1 under C is a faulty single subheading, for clearly additional headings under C are called for (for example, "Giving the child responsibilities during recess").

Often a faulty single subheading should be combined with the heading above it. Here is an example of such a faulty single subheading:

VOODOOISM IN THE UNITED STATES

    I. The practice of voodooism
      A. In New Orleans

If the writer intends to discuss only the voodooism in New Orleans, the first heading should be:

    I. The practice of voodooism in New Orleans

Such a faulty single subheading shows that the writer has not thought through the organization of the paper.

Although the majority of single subheadings in student outlines are faulty, a single subheading that presents just one example to illustrate a heading may properly be used. For example:

FAILURES IN SLUM-CLEARANCE PROGRAMS

    I. Effects of the impersonality of urban-renewal projects
      A. Rise in crime rates
      B. Wanton destruction of buildings
        1. Example: The Pruitt-Igor complex in St. Louis

To be sure that you and your readers understand any use you make of single subheadings, you should always try to introduce such a heading with the word *example*.

9
writing
the paper

WRITING THE FIRST DRAFT

Some Preliminaries

Before beginning to write your paper, you should have completed at least a rough version of your formal outline. The outline is especially important because it will help to provide the good organization that is a vital part of a term paper, and a good outline virtually assures good organization. Before you begin to write, you should also arrange your note cards in an order that corresponds to your outline. If you have labeled each note card with the Roman numeral it belongs under in the outline, you can work well in writing each segment of your paper covered by a first-level outline heading. If you have been able to add a second-level (capital-letter) outline heading as well, your work will be still easier. These steps are part of the standard procedure of writing a term paper. The more you depart from this procedure, the less likely you are to write a well-organized paper.

As you write your paper, keep your outline in sight and your note cards at hand to guide you in composing paragraphs. Keep your bibliography cards on your desk so that you can compose footnotes as needed. This textbook should also be on your desk so that you can verify footnote forms and other matters.

Your instructor will probably request that your finished paper be typewritten, but your first draft will be written in longhand. You will need to make revisions in your first draft before you type the finished paper. One method of revision is to write the whole paper in a first, or rough, draft and then to go back through it carefully, altering sentence structure, deleting useless material, and adding sentences as you see fit.

You may find, however, that an alternate method of revision, cumulative revision, will help you to rework your paper more thoroughly. Cumulative revision works this way: write three or four paragraphs; then pause and reread those paragraphs carefully, making as many improvements as you can. In all probability, you will find that you will need an additional sentence or a different wording to make an explanation clearer, or that you want to improve sentence structure, and so on. Once you have revised these paragraphs to your satisfaction, write another few paragraphs. After completing them, go back to the *beginning* of the paper and repeat the process, revising all that you have written. You will find that in your second reading of the first few paragraphs you will discover needed revisions that escaped your attention the first time through. Continue this process, returning to the *beginning* of the paper each time you have written three to six paragraphs. In a term paper of normal length, you might begin revision at the opening paragraph four to six times. If you use this method of cumulative revision, you will be amazed at the tautly organized results.

Writing the Introduction

The introduction of a term paper is usually longer than the introduction of a 500-word theme, which often consists of a single sentence. But the purpose of both introductions is the same: to announce the general subject matter of the paper and to attract the interest of the reader. The introduction should not be so dryly matter-of-fact that it causes little or no reaction in the reader, nor should it make use of suspenseful, folksy, human-interest, or teasing gimmicks in an effort to capture the reader's attention. The topic of the paper, stated in an uncontrived manner, should be enough to stir the reader's interest. You can make your introduction stylistically appealing by including in it a well-known allusion, or an impressive statement of fact, or a comment on an unusual situation, and so on. Chiefly, however, you want to lead your readers directly into the subject matter of your paper. A good introduction to a term paper will normally comprise six to twelve lines.

Here are two examples of term-paper introductions:

THE VIEWS ON BIRTH CONTROL HELD BY
LEADERS OF PROTESTANT CHURCHES

In the beginning, men and women were told, "Be fruitful and multiply, and fill the earth." Throughout the ages humanity has followed this first command of God so dutifully that today we are faced with a crucial decision. Now that we have "filled the earth" to its present overcrowded state, we may continue to multiply and thus perhaps face disaster, or we may impose birth control on the species. Everybody talks about the problem, but our church leaders are the ones most people look to for guidance and answers, for the problem has serious moral aspects.

This is a good term-paper introduction, for it specifies the drift of the paper's subject matter and does so in a tone and style that engage the reader's interest. The student has prepared her readers to consider the issue of birth control from the viewpoint of religious leaders. Note the allusion in the first sentence of the introduction; it is an attractive literary device, not merely a bid for attention. (Notice, too, that such a well-known, short quotation from the Bible should not be footnoted.)

A second example:

MARK TWAIN'S PHILOSOPHIC OUTLOOK
IN THE LAST DECADE OF HIS LIFE

After reading many of Mark Twain's works, one may wonder whether the person who wrote *Tom Sawyer* and *Huckleberry Finn* was really the same person who wrote *The Mysterious Stranger* and *Letters from Earth*. In philosophic tone and attitude the latter two works seem poles apart from the earlier works. But Mark Twain did indeed write all of these works. The apparent discrepancy in philosophic attitude is due to the change in Twain's intellectual outlook between his middle age and his latter years—a change from being a skeptical humorist to being a pessimistic, embittered social and religious critic. This paper will inquire into the causes of this change and the general results of it.

This, too, is a good introductory paragraph for a term paper. The problem the paper will examine is clearly established; the tone is straightforward and uncontrived. The reader is led to *want* to know the nature of Twain's intellectual metamorphosis. Since the student quoted Twain generously throughout the whole paper, she did not see the need for a pessimistic quotation in the introduction itself. Note that the last sentence of the introduction is virtually a thesis sentence. Such a sentence is not out of place. This type of sentence is used by many professional writers in such magazines as *Scientific American* and *The Sewanee Review.*

Once you have composed your introductory paragraph, you are ready to continue writing the paper, using your note cards and following your outline carefully. Before we discuss composition of the paper, we must consider two more preliminary points.

Entering Direct Quotations

The uses of direct quotations in term papers are discussed on pages 55–56. Review that material if necessary. Direct quotations are entered into term papers in three ways. If an ordinary direct quotation will occupy no more than four or at most five lines of text, it should be incorporated into the double-spaced text and enclosed in quotation marks, and it should be announced by an introductory tag. You should not abruptly enclose two or three sentences in quotation marks without announcing that a quotation is coming and indicating in some way its purpose.

Here is an example of the inclusion of a short direct quotation:

Meanwhile, demonstrations against and individual opposition to the use of defoliants in Vietnam were increasing in number and intensity. Important persons participated in the dissent. Wilfred Posnak, a noted botanist and plant geneticist, said that "the damage to the forests of South Vietnam is already so extensive that twenty years of natural growth will not restore that plant life to its normal state. Continued defoliation may destroy large portions of the forest forever."[4]

[4] "Herbicidal Warfare," *Current History* 52 (Sept. 1969), 540.

Note that (1) the quotation is short enough to be incorporated directly into the text; (2) an introductory tag leads into the quotation; (3) the purpose of the quotation—citing an authority—is made clear; (4) the footnote number comes directly after the final quotation marks; (5) the author's name, being given in full in the text, is not repeated in the footnote; and (6) since the quotation comes from a journal with continuous pagination throughout a volume year, the footnote form is that for a learned journal.

Some short quotations may be incorporated into the text but are not footnoted in the regular way. Short quotations from poems are an example of this sort and include a slash (/) to indicate where one line of poetry ends and another begins.

Here is an example of a short direct quotation without a footnote:

> In Section 52 of "Song of Myself," Whitman presents himself as being completely individualistic: "I too am not a bit tamed, I too am untranslatable, / I sound my barbaric yawp over the roofs of the world." (lines 1332–33)

If the title of the poem is not given in the introductory tag, it can be put in parentheses with the line numbers and no footnote is needed. If the number of lines of poetry quoted runs to four or more, they should be entered as an inset and footnoted in the regular way. Quotations from such well-known sources as the Bible, Shakespeare's plays, and dictionaries, when they make a point in the paper and are not used for literary embellishment, may be followed by their references enclosed in parentheses, such as (II Kings, 1: 28–29) or (*Hamlet,* III, ii, 12–14). Again, no footnote is needed.

The third method of entering direct quotations applies to quotations that occupy six or more lines in the paper. Such quotations are called insets because they are indented five spaces from the margin of the text.

Here is an example of an inset:

> Though wary of Indians in general, Francis Parkman did greatly admire some of their leaders, many of whom he felt to be fine and noble men. He was particularly impressed by an Oglala chief, describing him in these terms:
>
>> Mahto-Tatonka, in his way, was a hero. No chief could vie with him in warlike renown, or in power over his people. . . . He had a fearless spirit, and an impetuous and inflexible resolution. His will was law. He was politic and sagacious, and with true Indian craft, always befriended the whites, knowing that he might thus reap great advantages for himself and his adherents. When he had resolved on any course of conduct, he would pay to the warriors the compliment of calling them together to deliberate upon it, and when their debates were over, quietly state his own opinion, which no one ever disputed.[9]

---

[9] Parkman, p. 138.

84   Note that (1) the quotation occupies eleven lines, more than enough to warrant an inset; (2) quotation marks do *not* enclose the quotation; (3) the first line's lack of extra indentation means that the quotation does not come from the beginning of a paragraph (if it did, the first line would be indented ten spaces instead of five); (4) in addition to the five-space indentation on the left there is a slightly wider margin on the right; (5) the inset is single spaced; (6) the four spaced periods, called an ellipsis, indicate that one or more sentences have been omitted because they were not relevant (three spaced periods would indicate the omission of just part of the interior of a sentence); (7) the quotation is properly introduced by an introductory tag; and (8) the purpose of the quotation is to present direct evidence for the point made about Parkman's admiration of some Indians.

Entering Footnotes in the First Draft

While writing your paper you should compose footnotes as they are needed. If you wait until you finish the paper to compose them, you are more likely to make errors. You will cause yourself the inconvenience of searching through your note cards to find bibliography card numbers, and you will run the risk of mistakenly including the wrong reference.

If your footnotes are to be at the bottom of the page (many, if not most, instructors require this method) you should not put them at the bottom of the page in your first draft. Instead, draw a line across your paper immediately beneath the line of longhand containing the footnote number. Compose the footnote at that point, draw a second line across the paper beneath the footnote, and continue writing. When you type your paper, this simple method will allow you to judge the space needed for footnotes for a particular page. When you type the final draft, you will be able to tell at a glance how many footnotes will be on any one page. (Refer to page 62 for instructions on how to use a guide sheet to tell how much space you need to reserve for footnotes on a page.)

Here is an example of how to enter footnotes in your first draft:

THE EMERGENCE OF AN INDEPENDENT CONGO

The Congo became an official Belgian colony in 1908. At that time the Congolese saw their situation improve dramatically. They enjoyed greater individual freedom, a better educational system, and better political administration.[1] King

---

[1] Washington Okum, *Lumumba's Congo* (New York: Ivan Obolensky, 1963), p. 16.

Leopold II had ruled for twenty-three years the country ironically called the Congo Free State. During this time the

Congolese had been enslaved and had suffered many atrocities, all with the approval of the King. The country's population declined so rapidly that officials in 1960 estimated that the population of 14,000,000 numbered 6,000,000 less than the population in 1885.[2]

85

---

[2] Ibid., p. 14.

The Congo remained a Belgian colony until . . . .

5

910.03
0 57

Washington Okum, Lumumba's Congo,

New York, Ivan Obolensky, Inc., 1963

bibliography card

I   5

Had been ruled 23 years by King Leopold II as Congo Free State. People had been enslaved. Atrocities committed, approved by the King. Population had declined. About 6,000,000 less in 1960 (14,000,000) than in 1885.

pp. 14 and 16 — Millions tortured and slaughtered. / Improvement began after status of colony was established in 1908. Better administration. Improved educational system. More freedom.

note card

Note that (1) number 5 on the note card permits an accurate footnote to be composed from bibliography card 5; (2) Roman numeral I tells that this information should go into the first part of the paper; (3) the notes are condensed; (4) expansion of the notes helped the student to avoid plagiarism; (5) a slash on the note card indicates the end of page 14, and shows that the remaining notes came from page 16 (pp. 14 and 16 differ from pp. 14–16 in that pp. 14–16 also include page 15); (6) footnotes set off by lines at the exact place the footnoted material occurs will make typing much easier; and (8) that the short form "ibid." plus page number serves as the second footnote.

Developing Unified Paragraphs from Outline Headings

Students writing term papers have sufficient notes and plenty of facts and ideas to write about, but too often they assimilate their information into overlong and disunified paragraphs. Paragraphs should be kept to a length of 75 to 150 words. A shorter paragraph, unless it is transitional, is usually fragmentary. Longer paragraphs are fatiguing to readers. An ideal paragraph would be one in which a topic sentence is developed either by details or analysis, or both. In real-life writing, however, textbook paragraphs are uncommon. Paragraphs vary greatly according to styles of writing. Shorter paragraphs such as those characterized by newspaper writing offer compact development of ideas. Longer paragraphs such as those found in philosophical discourses present meticulously developed complex ideas.

Your outline is your guide to paragraph composition. Remember that outline headings are capsule summaries of parts of your paper, not specifics. No outline heading should be so specific as to cover only one sentence in your paper. A third-level heading will often cover just one paragraph. A second-level heading may cover two or more paragraphs, and of course a first-level heading may cover several paragraphs. *An outline heading that covers more than one paragraph will be served by only one topic sentence.*

Suppose that a particular second-level heading in your outline requires about 300 words for proper development. The outline heading itself contains the idea that will be converted into the topic sentence for the subject to be discussed, but a 300-word paragraph is too long for a typical term paper. Therefore you will have two or three paragraph indentations in your 300-word development of the second-level heading; and one topic sentence will serve the whole segment of two or three paragraphs. Divide the 300-word segment at a natural breaking point and start a new paragraph at each of those breaking points. Almost every 300-word segment of writing will have at least one and perhaps two points where a new paragraph can begin without disturbing the smooth unity of the whole.

Weaknesses occur in the paragraphing of many term papers because students either have a flawed outline or fail to let a good outline guide their paragraph development. The result is often an over-long paragraph that should be divided or a disunified paragraph that contains material from two or more outline headings. Follow your outline closely as you compose your paper. Understand that each of its headings will need at least one full paragraph of explanation and that often the development of a second- or first-level heading will call for two or more paragraph indentations, with each starting at a natural breaking point where a smooth transition can be made from one paragraph to the next, even though both are developing a topic sentence based on one outline heading. *Never* write one paragraph that covers more than one outline heading.

Following is an example of how a student produced flawed paragraphing because he did not follow his outline carefully. First, here is a segment of his outline:

THE SOVIET EDUCATIONAL REFORM
MOVEMENT OF 1958

V. Reasons for the failure of the reform movement
   A. Ineffective administration of the program
   B. Failure to achieve the stated goals
   C. The program's disregard of general education

This is reasonably good outlining. Heading B might have had third-level headings under it, but they certainly are not necessary. The student should have realized that heading V would become a topic sentence and that at least three paragraphs corresponding to headings A, B, and C were needed. He should also have been alert to the need to break one or more of the capital-letter headings into two or more paragraph indentations. Here is what he produced for this segment of his outline:

The failure of the reform movement was now apparent to many. From the beginning there had been great difficulty in administering the program. The criticism and complaints of the Soviet citizens prevented the educational commissars from attaining their goal of having no more than 50 percent of Soviet students in secondary schools so that vocational training would increase. The lowest figure ever reached was 64 percent in 1960.[23]* (*The writer has already entered mate-*

* No text will accompany footnotes, for we are concerned here with the actual writing of the paper rather than with documentation.

rial belonging to heading B before he has developed heading A to any extent.) It remained clear that the large majority of the students wanted an academic rather than a vocational education, even though salaries of professionals were no higher than those of workers.[24] The administrators of the program tried to change the public attitude, but could not succeed. The lack of an adequate supply of well-trained labor teachers was also a dilemma for the administrators: if people were taken out of production to teach, the purpose of the reform would be defeated. Not only did the administrators disregard general education, they failed to meet their vocational goals as well. (*By now the writer has introduced aspects of headings A, B, and C into one paragraph. His paragraph is now long enough, but he continues.*) Furthermore, because the school system depended on industry to provide facilities, labor education became a burden to industry. Conflicts between the educators and the managers of industry increased.[25] Morale among students was low. Many resorted to cheating in order to escape vocational training and gain admission into academic programs.[26] (*By its end, the paragraph's unity is hopelessly lost; the student has been haphazardly stringing sentences together without following his outline.*)

Aside from the difficulty of administering the new program, the reform did not achieve its stated goals. (*The opening sentence of this paragraph implies that this paragraph will deal only with the subject matter of heading B. But not so.*) Due to several factors, the economic problem persisted. Money was wasted and poorly trained students were the rule rather than the exception.[27] Because there was no coordination between the educational reform program and the rapid development of Soviet technology, the skills taught were often obsolete by the time a student graduated. (*This point belongs under heading A and, being out of place, produces paragraph disunity.*) This was due mainly to importation of new technological methods from the West, chiefly from the United States.[28] Ideological effects of the reform also fell below the expectations of the Party. The program failed to rid Soviet society of "educational elitism" because special schools reserved for gifted students became "hideouts" for children of influential parents. Parents with influence made sure that the two-year labor requirement did not apply to their children.[29] But in spite of the efforts of so many to avoid the vocational training and to enter academic studies, the reform program's disregard of general education was causing a decline in the achievement of the most gifted students. (*Now heading C is being introduced into the second paragraph, further increasing paragraph disunity.*) There was much criticism of the academic lag caused by overburdening the students, eliminating incentive, and not providing sufficient

instruction in traditional education.[30] In spite of all these failures the reformers pressed ahead with their plans. By the
1961–1962 school year they had decided that the secondary-
school course would be cut from three to two years so that
more time could be denoted to "production practice."[31]
*(Material that does not even belong under heading V further
disrupts paragraph unity.)* By 1965, however, it was announced that the two-year labor requirement would no longer
be a prerequisite for university entrance.[32] Failure of the reform was being recognized, and the way was being prepared
for a return to traditional educational practices.

This student writer violated the principles of good paragraphing both by
writing overlong paragraphs and by destroying paragraph unity by
mixing subject matter from three distinctly different outline headings
into one paragraph. In fact, materials from headings A, B, and C are
mixed in each of his two overlong, disunified paragraphs. His poor results were due chiefly to his stringing sentences together without
regard for the unity they should produce in a paragraph—a very
common weakness in term papers. This student apparently thought
that if he took sentences from various sources and put them together
his paper would sound learned, and the charge of plagiarism could not
be lodged against him. A check of his sources, incidentally, revealed
that many of his sentences were almost identical in wording to sentences from his sources. His paper was not only disjointed but pla-
giarized.

Refer again to the outline segment on page 87. A second writer
took notes from the sources used to provide information for the flawed
paragraphs above and composed from them the following unified paragraphs, which follow the outline headings exactly.

The failure of the Soviet educational reform movement was
due to three main causes. First, the program was so ineptly
administered as to make its success all but impossible. A sufficient number of trained labor teachers was never available
because industry could not spare its most talented workers to
be transferred to the educational sector. And the labor teachers who were on the job found that their supplies and equip-
ment were improperly ordered or not delivered at all. The
planners did not coordinate their work properly.[23] The
planners also were too zealous in their desire for ideological
indoctrination so that too much time was consumed by political lectures and too little devoted to classroom education and
vocational training.[24] A student of the educational reform
movement can only conclude that the age-old weaknesses of a
top-heavy bureaucracy prevented even the sincere reformers

from performing their duties adequately. (*Outline heading A has been sufficiently covered in this one unified paragraph; no extraneous material has been introduced in the paragraph.*)

But perhaps the clearest evidence that the reform program was a failure is that its stated goals were not achieved. (*The first sentence of this paragraph is a topic sentence for outline heading B.*) The foremost goal of the planners was to indoctrinate the public with the attitude that vocational training and manual labor were to enjoy a status equal to that of academic education and professional work. That program of indoctrination failed. Students could not be persuaded not to aim for higher academic education. Many resorted to cheating to insure their entry into secondary schools and universities.[25] Influential parents were able to prevent the two-year labor requirement from applying to their children. The desired transformation of public attitudes toward education was not achieved.[26]

(*The writer saw the need for two paragraph indentations for heading B. He chose a natural breaking point to begin his second paragraph.*)

Furthermore, the labor training which was so heavily emphasized as a part of the reform program did not produce the desired results. The quality of vocational training declined rather than improved. One economic expert stated that "it has become increasingly evident that production training has turned out hundreds of thousands of rather poorly trained young people—low-grade and semiskilled personnel whose training costs were completely wasted in the economic sense because very few of them would . . . be engaged in those trades for which they were trained."[27] Many of the skills taught were obsolete by the time the students were to become workers. This was due to the fact that Soviet technology, borrowing heavily from Western methods, was advancing more rapidly than the educational program.[28] (*Two unified paragraphs have covered heading B.*)

A third cause of the program's failure was its disregard of general education. (*The phrasing of the topic sentence of this paragraph tells the reader that heading C will be developed in a unified paragraph.*) Soviet educators admitted that general education and academic standards had suffered. In 1961, for example, 112,000 of 227,000 secondary-school graduates failed the university entrance exams, the largest percentage of failures ever recorded during the Soviet regime. More than one-third of evening students did not complete their courses, and the dropout rate in academic courses rose to the highest level.[29] It became evident that not only were the stated goals of the reform program not achieved but that the benefits of the traditional educational system of the past was being lost.

This writer did not just string sentences together with little regard for the **91** connection between them but maintained unity in his paragraphs by having all the sentences in each paragraph pertain to the central idea of that paragraph, which is stated in one of the outline headings.

Maintaining Coherence Between and Within Paragraphs

Although unity and coherence are closely allied, they represent two different characteristics of writing. The following pair of sentences illustrates this point:

Today, Henry Fielding's *Tom Jones* is called a novel. Fielding called it a "comic epic in prose."

These two sentences certainly belong together and are thus unified. Within a full paragraph describing what kind of book *Tom Jones* is, neither could possibly produce disunity. Yet full coherence between the two sentences is lacking. The reader feels something of a jar or disruption while passing from the first sentence to the second. Note how much the simple connective *but* adds to the sentences by joining them into a single, compound sentence:

Today, Henry Fielding's *Tom Jones* is called a novel, but Fielding called it a "comic epic in prose."

Smoothness has replaced the disruptive effect that was caused by the lack of the connective *but*. Coherence has made unity more apparent.

The word *coherence* comes from the Latin *co*, meaning "together," and from the Latin *haerere*, meaning "to stick." Thus coherence literally means "a sticking together." It is a quality that makes writing integrated, consistent, smooth, and intelligible. These characteristics result when parts of sentences, sentences, and paragraphs "stick together," or have smooth transition between them.

Coherence is achieved in several ways. An obvious way is the use of connectives, as illustrated by the connective *but* in the example above. English has dozens of connectives that express relationships between ideas and provide smooth transition between short or long passages of writing. They include such words and phrases as *also, and, yet, therefore, for example, in addition, however,* and so on.

Coherence may also be effected by the repetition in one sentence of a key word from the previous sentence. Note that the following sentences, though possessing unity, lack coherence.

The adventures of Tom Jones are mostly earthy, bawdy, and rollicking. He has an affair with a woman believed to be his mother.

Notice that the repetition of a key word provides full coherence between the sentences:

The adventures of Tom Jones are mostly earthy, bawdy, and rollicking. In one such adventure he has an affair with a woman believed to be his mother.

The repetition of *adventure* provides the glue of coherence.

A third common method of achieving coherence is the use of a pronoun in one sentence to refer to a noun or idea in the preceding sentence. For example:

Tom established an alliance with a promiscuous upperclass woman in London. She provided him with opportunities for advancement.

The use of *she* to refer to *woman* and *him* to refer to *Tom* produces coherence. You will see the value of this coherence, when you read the sentences below:

Tom established an alliance with a promiscuous upperclass woman in London. Opportunities for advancement were provided.

The ideas remain but the coherence vanishes, making the writing poor.

Other characteristics of writing, such as close relationship of ideas and parallelism of sentence structure, also contribute to coherence. But use of connectives, repetition of key words, and use of pronoun reference are the most obvious means of achieving coherence and are the ones that you should pay most attention to.

The necessity for coherence is not limited only to clauses within a single sentence. Each sentence must lead logically to another just as each paragraph must proceed meaningfully to the next, until the entire research paper has evolved. Lack of proper coherence is common in research papers because many students, when gathering together ideas from various sources, often fail to make clear the relationships between their sentences; that is, they fail to make the sentences—and paragraphs too—stick together. Not only must the ideas in consecutive sentences be in proper order but the way in which the sentences are related to each other must be made clear as well—both coherence and unity are necessary.

Here, from a student research paper, is an example of insufficiently coherent writing:

THE ROLE OF ARTIFICIAL SATELLITES
IN COMMUNICATIONS

Active satellites entered the world scene with the successful launching of Courier IB on October 10, 1960. Messages were sent from a ground station and stored on a tape recorder. Retransmission occurred on another part of the globe. Performance went well for seventeen days; malfunction caused operations to cease.

The first commercial communications satellite, Telstar I, went up on July 10, 1962, and was designed and built by Bell Telephone Laboratories. The first transmission of television signals occurred between the United States and Europe. Six days later color television signals were relayed. It contained 3600 solar cells charging nineteen nickel-cadmium batteries. The earth was orbited once every two and one-half hours. Like previous satellites, Telstar I was in common view of earth stations for only brief periods of time because of its relatively low altitude of 3000 miles. Syncom II solved this problem. With a stationary orbit 22,300 miles up, a much wider range of transmission was possible.

Ironically, the chief reason that this passage has so little coherence is that the student changed the structure of sentences in his sources in order to avoid plagiarism. In doing this he did not, as he wrote a sentence, keep in mind his preceding sentence, and severely diminished coherence resulted.

Here is the passage rewritten, with some of the means of providing coherence italicized:

Satellites that could receive and retransmit messages entered the world scene with the successful launching of Courier IB on October 10, 1960. A ground station transmitted radio messages to *Courier IB, where they* were stored on a tape recorder. *Retransmission* of the *messages* back to earth occurred on another part of the globe. *Courier IB's* performance went well for seventeen days; then a malfunction *in the satellite* caused *its* operations to cease.

Less than two years after *Courier IB's* success, the first commercial communications satellite, Telstar I, designed and built by Bell Telephone Laboratories, was launched. The first transmission of television signals via *Telstar I* occurred between the United States and Europe shortly after the *satellite* was launched on July 10, 1962. Six days *later* color *television* signals were relayed via *Telstar I.*

Telstar I was powered by 3600 solar cells charging nineteen nickel-cadmium batteries. *It* orbited the earth every two and one-half hours. Like previous satellites, *it* was in common view of earth stations for only brief periods of time because of *its* relatively low altitude of 3000 miles. The rapidity of *its* orbiting limited *its* use as a relay station. *But this* problem was solved by Syncom II, which had a stationary *orbit* 22,300 miles up. Such a high *stationary orbit* gave *that satellite* a much wider range of transmission than that of *Telstar I.*

Now, because of the use of connectives, repetition of key words, and use of pronoun reference, the passage is coherent and much easier to understand than the original.

As you write a sentence, keep the preceding sentence in mind so that you can properly relate the two. You be certain, too, that there is proper transition from one paragraph to the next. Maintaining coherence in term papers is difficult because you will often use in one paragraph materials from several sources. Yet if you think about each sentence as you write it, you can make it "stick" to the preceding sentence and thus maintain coherence.

Tables and Illustrations

Occasionally a term paper—especially one dealing with a technical topic—will contain tables or illustrations. These should be entered into the paper in an orderly, clearly understandable way.

A table is a systematic arrangement of statistics in columns. Here is an example:

Table II

POLITICAL POLL OF STUDENTS ON THE
CHIEF PROBLEM THE COUNTRY NOW FACES

	Republicans	Democrats	Independents
1. Inept presidential administration	4	66	32
2. Incompetent Congress	43	12	17
3. Excessive power of trade unions	62	36	31
4. Collusion among large corporations	12	55	29
5. Decline of morality among the people	28	22	8

The table number and its title are given above the table.

SUBJECTIVE CASE	OBJECTIVE CASE	POSSESSIVE CASE
I	me	my, mine
we	us	our, ours
you		your, yours
he	him	his
she	her	hers
it		its
they	them	their, theirs
who	whom	whose

ENGLISH PRONOUN CASE FORMS

Figure 1

Any kind of chart, graph, diagram, drawing, photograph, map, and so on, that is not a table is in research papers referred to as an illustration. The title of an illustration is listed below the illustration and is labeled as "Figure 1," "Figure 2," and so on. Here are two examples:

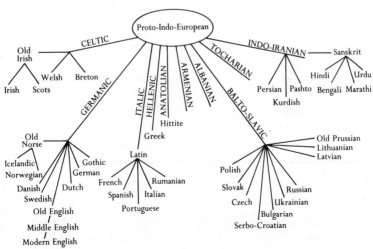

INDO-EUROPEAN LANGUAGE FAMILY TREE

Figure 2

Follow these directions when you enter tables and illustrations in your term paper:

1 Be sure your table or illustration is accurate and easily interpretable. Make it as simple and brief as possible.
2 Use Roman numerals for table numbers and Arabic numerals for figure numbers—for example, Table V, Figure 5.
3 Always have a caption or title for each table and illustration and put the caption above the table but below the illustration.
4 Capitalize captions, but capitalize only the first letter of "Table" and "Figure."
5 Number tables consecutively and illustrations consecutively. Do not merge the numbers of the two types; do not have such a sequence as Figure 4, Table V, and Figure 6.
6 Leave a double space both above and below each table or illustration.
7 Center the label of a table two spaces above the caption of the table, which will be above the table. Center the label of an illustration two spaces below the caption of the illustration, which will be below the illustration.
8 When possible, place a table or illustration at the point in the text where it is discussed, but not before your first reference to it. If an illustration is quite large, however, put it on a separate sheet of paper. In such a case it should still be referred to by table number or figure number.
9 When referring in the text to a table or illustration, be sure to make the significance of the entry clear but do not explain what a glance at the table or illustration itself makes completely obvious. Avoid repeating in the text too many of the statistics in a table or illustration.
10 When referring in the text to a table or illustration, you may mention the page as well as the table or illustration number, for example, "Figure 4, page 9." Avoid such imprecise phrases as "the preceding table" or "the illustration below."
11 If you need to footnote a table or illustration, use an asterisk after the table or illustration number, such as Figure 6*—a footnote number might be confused with the figure number. Use an asterisk at the bottom of the page to introduce the footnote. If two such footnotes are needed on one page, use one asterisk for the first and two asterisks for the second.

Writing the Conclusion

While the conclusion of a 500-word theme is often just a single sentence, the conclusion of a term paper normally occupies a full paragraph. The concluding paragraph need not review all the details of the paper, but it should summarize any overall conclusion its author has drawn, even if that conclusion has been made clear in the paper. As a summary, the conclusion should express the totality of the subject matter of the paper. From reading only the concluding paragraph, a reader should be able to get an accurate idea of what has been said in the term paper.

In addition, the concluding paragraph should *sound* like a conclusion and not just be an abrupt end of the paper. There should be a note of finality in it. The readers should be made to feel that they have read a *complete* paper.

Here is a good concluding paragraph from a research paper entitled "Albert Einstein's Philosophical Religion":

> Thus we see that Einstein's religion was not a religion in the usual meaning of the word. His religion had no name, no creed, no followers. It was an individual code of life for a solitary man. He did not concern himself with personal salvation or the details of creeds and isms. But he was deeply religious in the highest sense, with a profound conviction of the unity of nature and of the presence of purpose in the universe. In his mind there was only one God, and he sought him by exploring the endless mysteries of nature and the ordered universe.

From this concluding paragraph a reader can rather closely guess what the text of the paper has said. The reader also *feels* the completion of the paper. A good conclusion should have these qualities.

TYPING THE FINISHED PAPER

If you have used the method of cumulative revision described on page 80, you should be ready to type your paper as soon as you have finished your final cumulative revision.

The checklist below is for your guidance. Put a check mark by each number to indicate that you have adhered to its directions.

Some Technical Aspects of Typing

1 Use 20-pound bond typing paper, if possible. Since most college libraries now have machines that make copies inexpensively, it should not be necessary to type a carbon copy.
2 Type your paper with double spacing, except for inset quotations, footnotes, and bibliographic entries. Double space between individual footnotes and bibliographic entries.

3 Double space after colons and after periods, question marks, and exclamation points that close sentences. If a sentence ends with a set of quotation marks or a parenthesis, use double spacing after those marks. Leave only a single space after all other marks of punctuation, including periods after abbreviations.

4 Maintain a margin of at least one inch but no more than one and one-quarter inches at the top, bottom, and left side of the page. The margin on the right side will be uneven but should be as close to one inch as possible. Avoid extra-wide margins.

5 Indent inset quotations five spaces and single space them. Indicate whether or not the inset quotation is the beginning of a paragraph.

6 Use three spaced periods (. . .) to show an omission in the interior of a sentence of a direct quotation. Use four spaced periods (. . . .) if the omission includes the end of a sentence or more than one sentence.

7 To make the Arabic numeral 1 use the small letter l, not the capital I. Capital I makes the Roman numeral I.

8 Use two hyphens (--) to make a dash and leave no space before or after a dash. Do not mistake the underlining mark (_) for a dash. Do not use a dash as a mark of end punctuation.

9 In underlining titles of more than one word, use continuous underlining unless your instructor requests you not to underline the blank spaces.

10 To enter raised (superior) numbers for footnotes, turn the carriage roller frontwards half a space, type your number, and then return the roller to its original setting.

11 Leave no space before a footnote number in the text or after a footnote number in the footnote itself.

12 Do not leave a space after a first parenthesis or before the closing parenthesis.

13 When enumerating several items, use Arabic numerals within parentheses, as follows: A colon may be used (1) after the salutation in a formal letter; (2) after an introductory label; (3) after a noun that introduces a series; (4) after a sentence that is followed by a sentence of explanation; and (5) after a phrase or sentence that introduces a long direct quotation.

14 Underline foreign words and phrases that have not become Anglicized.

15 Follow the rules given in any standard handbook for capitalization, punctuation, the use of abbreviations, and the use of Arabic numerals and spelled-out numbers.

The Title Page

1 Do not put a blank sheet of paper before your title page if your paper is enclosed in a folder.

2 Your title page should contain (1) the title, (2) your name in a "by" **99** phrase, (3) the course name, and (4) your instructor's name.
3 You may use the titles Professor, Mr., Mrs., Miss, or Ms. with your instructor's name.
4 The four pieces of information in number 2 above should be carefully centered on the title page.

The Outline

1 The title of your paper should be repeated at the top of your outline page(s) and the heading "Outline" should be centered on the third line below the title. The thesis sentence precedes the first heading of the outline.
2 Leave a margin of at least one inch but no more than one and one-quarter inches at the left side of the page.
3 Indent second-level headings five spaces and third-level headings ten spaces.
4 Before typing your outline, check carefully to see that it adheres to the principles of formal outlining discussed in Chapter 8.

Footnotes at the Bottom of the Page

1 Use a guide sheet as described on page 62 to be sure you have the proper amount of space for the footnotes on any one page.
2 Type a two- to three-inch line between the text and the footnotes on any one page. Double space above and below the line.
3 Indent the first line of a footnote five spaces but type additional lines flush left with the text.
4 Single space each footnote but double space between footnotes.
5 Use raised footnote numbers; do not put a period after a footnote number.
6 Leave no space after the raised footnote number.
7 Be sure that every footnote entry follows exactly the appropriate form as given in Chapter 7.
8 Use short footnote forms as illustrated in Chapter 7.
9 The sample research paper in Chapter 10 illustrates the eight points above.

Footnotes at the End of the Paper

1 If your instructor asks you to enter your footnotes at the end of your paper, type them on a separate page or pages.

2 Center the heading "Footnotes" on the first page.

3 Maintain a margin of at least one inch but no more than one and one-quarter inches.

4 Use raised numbers, not numbers followed by periods.

5 Indent and space the footnotes in the same manner as bottom-of-the-page footnotes (see page 99).

6 Put the page(s) of footnotes between the end of the paper and the formal bibliography.

7 The sample critical paper in Chapter 10 illustrates the six points above.

The Bibliography

1 Type your formal bibliography on a separate page or pages.

2 Center the heading "Bibliography" at the top of the first page.

3 Maintain a margin of at least one inch but no more than one and one-quarter inches.

4 Single space each bibliography entry but double space between entries.

5 Leave a margin of one to one and one-quarter inches and indent all subsequent lines in each item five spaces.

6 Present your bibliography in one alphabetized list with anonymous sources entered by the first word of the title (except *a*, *an*, and *the*); do not use the word anonymous.

7 If an author has two or more bibliographic entries, substitute for his or her name after its first use a long dash (_____).

8 Be sure that each entry follows exactly the appropriate form as given in Chapter 7.

9 The sample papers in Chapter 10 illustrate the eight points above.

Pagination

Number pages consecutively from your outline (page 1) to the final page of the bibliography. Do not number outline, footnote, or bibliography pages separately.

Proofreading

After you have typed your paper, proofread it carefully. Proofread footnotes and bibliographic entries twice. Make corrections neatly.

Folder

Unless your instructor gives you different directions, submit your paper in a clasp folder with the paper's title and your name on the outside of the folder.

10
sample
term papers

The first term paper in this chapter is a research paper. The student gathered source materials and fashioned them into an organized whole that presents some essential information about the therapeutic uses of music. The student did not make original observations about her subject but organized the results of her research into an original term paper.

The second term paper in this chapter is a documented critical paper. The student did some research in secondary sources to provide background material for the main part of his paper, which consists of his own interpretation of *The Red Badge of Courage,* by Stephen Crane. He did not just present the results of his research but contributed his own evaluation of a work of literature.

The two papers have important differences, but the two students used nearly identical procedures in preparing their papers. Study of

102   these papers will help you understand better the standard procedure of writing term papers that is discussed in Chapters 1–9.

The research paper illustrates placement of footnotes at the bottom of pages, and the critical paper illustrates placement of footnotes at the end of the paper.

The comments in
the margins point
out aspects of term-
paper writing de-
scribed in the text-
book.

THERAPEUTIC USES OF MUSIC

by

Katherine Morton

See page 98 for in-
structions on com-
posing and typing
the title page.

English 1A

Professor Roberta Sanders

May 10, 1974

1

THERAPEUTIC USES OF MUSIC

Outline

The thesis sentence, which precedes the first heading of the outline, states the central idea of the paper.

Thesis sentence: Because of its psychological and physiological effects on individuals and groups, music has therapeutic uses in the treatment of mental and physical illnesses.

This outline is properly balanced, and each heading refers to a general point presented in the paper.

I. The psychological and physiological effects of music

    A. Psychological responses to music

        1. In individuals

        2. In groups

    B. Physical responses to music

For a discussion of writing the formal outline, see Chapter 8 (p. 71).

II. Music therapy in ancient times

III. The use of music for psychotherapy in modern times

    A. To reduce abnormal self-centeredness

See page 99 for instructions on typing the formal outline.

    B. To alter undesirable moods

        1. The "iso" principle of suiting music to mood

        2. The encouragement of patients to participate in producing music

    C. To reach apparently inaccessible patients

    D. To assist in group therapy

    E. To abate senility

IV. The use of music therapy for resocialization

V. The use of music for physical therapy

    A. To relieve patients whose physical injuries lead them to despair

    B. To help rehabilitate patients with brain damage

2

      1. The use of Musicall, a simplified method of teaching music

      2. Other uses of music therapy in physical rehabilitation of

         brain-damaged patients

   C. To help rehabilitate polio victims

VI. Present trends in use and evaluation of music therapy

sample term papers

THERAPEUTIC USES OF MUSIC

Many kinds of mental and physical ailments plague the human race, and many kinds of therapy are needed to treat these ailments. In the past few decades, medical and paramedical practitioners have begun to use music as therapy in treating both mental and physical debilities. Though results in the therapeutic use of music have not been consistent, successes have been numerous enough to establish some valid generalizations, and progress has been made in understanding how music produces its therapeutic effects. This paper will inquire into the nature and success of the use of music therapy.

To use music therapy, a practitioner must understand the psychological and physiological effects of music on individuals and groups. An individual's emotional response to music is largely conditioned, for the music enjoyed by one generation is often rejected by another generation; for example, the rock music that excited the youth of the 1960s and '70s often irritated older generations. But once an individual learns to respond to numerous kinds of music in a variety of emotional ways, the responses are always evoked in the nervous system.

Ira M. Altshuler, a psychiatrist who has used music therapy, maintains that, unlike verbal communication, which follows a cerebrum-thalamus-cerebrum pathway, music is perceived first by the thalamus, which then sends impulses to the cerebrum. According to Altshuler, the thalamus-cerebrum pathway enables music to evoke emotional or psychological reactions when words will not and to produce more subconscious reactions than words. He thinks, in fact, that music can produce a response when nothing else can.[1]

------

[1]"A Psychiatrist's Experience with Music as a Therapeutic Agent," in _Music and Medicine_, ed. Dorothy M. Schullian and Max Schoen (New York: Henry Schuman, 1948), pp. 271-72.

The style of the introduction is straightforward and uncontrived. The final sentence is virtually a thesis sentence.

See pages 80–82 for a discussion of writing the introduction.

In a footnote at the bottom of the page, omit the author's name if his or her full name has appeared in the footnoted passage.

Refer to footnote forms on pages 63–66 to be sure that your footnotes contain the necessary information and follow the proper form.

4

If Altshuler is right, it would seem obvious that music has special therapeutic powers.

Other writers disagree with Altshuler, however, and maintain that both
music and verbal communication follow the same cerebrum-thalamus-cerebrum
pathway. Music's effects, they assert, are primarily due to association;
that is, people respond to music according to what they associate the music
with.[2] If music does produce responses chiefly through association, the
technical manner in which music affects the mind--its neural pathway--is not
important to the therapist, who would need to determine what effects various
kinds of music produce in various patients. Thus music's therapeutic powers
are limited unless the therapist is aware of the musical preferences of a
particular patient.

Most commentators agree that three important psychological effects of
music play the major roles in music therapy. First, music can distract
patients so that they forget their pain or disturbed state of mind.[3] The
second important psychological effect is that music can capture a person's
attention.[4] At first this effect might seem to be the opposite of distrac-
tion, but it is actually complementary, for a patient who is distracted from
pain or a disturbed mood can give full attention to a therapist. The third
important effect is that music can alter moods.[5]

Music not only affects individuals in individual ways but has the
power to affect groups as well. This is chiefly due to the fact that music

---

[2]Juliette Alvin, _Music Therapy_ (New York: Humanities Press, 1966),
pp. 89-90.

[3]Charles Fowler, "The Noise That Banishes Pain," _Popular Electronics_,
Jan. 1961, p. 50.

[4]Altshuler, p. 272.

[5]Doris Soibelman, _Therapeutic and Industrial Uses of Music_ (New York:
Columbia Univ. Press, 1948), p. 96.

See page 99 for in-
structions on en-
tering and typing
footnotes for your
paper.

The form used in
footnote 4 is a
short form that
refers to the work
cited in footnote 1.
Since only one
work by Altshuler
has been cited, his
name and the page
number make the
short form.

is the most social of all the arts, and that music is usually produced by
and for groups. According to Alvin, music produces psychological responses
in groups in the same way that it does in individuals--through association.[6]
Because music can affect groups, it has been used in group therapy.

People respond to music physically as well as psychologically. Music
can influence respiration, pulse rate, blood pressure, and muscle contrac-
tion.[7] These effects are probably related to music's ability to distract
and alter moods. Music can also spark uncontrollable reflexes, influence
the electrical conductivity of the body, cause nerves to discharge, and
incite subconscious responses to rhythm, such as toe-tapping.[8] These effects
are probably related to music's ability to distract and to capture attention.
But no one seems to know what role music's physical effects play in mental
or physical therapy.

Music as therapy is not new. References in the Bible show that music
was used in ancient times for healing purposes. For example, the story of David
calming the afflicted Saul is told in I Samuel, xvi: 23. There are also
many other recorded accounts of music used as therapy in ancient times, both
in healing by magic and by supposedly scientific practices.[9] In the ancient
world, music was primarily used to calm disturbed patients. Many practitioners thought music helped to exorcise evil demons that possessed their
patients.

In industrialized and science-oriented Western countries, however,
music therapy has not been used to any extent until comparatively recently.

Additional short
forms for subse-
quent references
are described on
pages 66–67.

[6]Alvin, p. 97.

[7]Charles M. Diserens, "The Development of an Experimental Psychology
of Music," in Music and Medicine, p. 384.

[8]S. V. Beavers, "Hospital Music Clinic," Recreation, 56 (Dec. 1963),
479.

[9]Alvin, pp. 27, 33, 42, 63.

6

It is used most often to treat mental rather than physical disorders,
though it is sometimes difficult to separate the two. In many cases, mental
patients are abnormally self-centered. A program of music therapy can often
help such patients to shift their attention away from themselves, thus
causing them to forget their problems momentarily. Over a period of time,
a patient may receive relief, but such cases are uncommon.[10]

Even when mental patients are not abnormally self-centered, music may
successfully alter some of their undesirable moods, such as anxiety, depression, fear, and so one. Since the duration of the altered mood varies from
patient to patient, no consistently effective kind of music therapy has
been developed.[11] Nonetheless many successes have been reported. In at-
tempting to alter undesirable moods, practitioners try to match the music to
the mood they want to change. This pairing of music to mood is known as
the "iso" principle, the idea being first to attract the patient's attention
and then gradually to change the mood to a desirable one. For example, a
depressed patient's attention might be attracted by somber music and then a
gay and lively piece might be played to alter the mood. Or a hyperactive
patient's attention might be attracted by loud, fast music, and the hyper-
activity might then be subdued by slower music.[12]

One commentator suggested that Mozart's music is best for calming disturbed patients.[13] Following this lead, a practitioner went so far as to
recommend specific composers and specific musical forms for certain purposes.
He suggested Beethoven's adagios to reduce hysteria or cure insomnia, allegros

---

[10]Charles W. Hughes, "Rhythm and Health," in Music and Medicine, p. 185.

[11]Diserens, p. 381.

[12]Altshuler, p. 272.

[13]"Music to Not Listen To" in "After Hours," Harper's, Nov. 1956, p. 82.

The student achieves coherence between paragraphs by repeating a key idea from the previous paragraph.

Coherence between and within paragraphs is discussed on pages 91–94.

to cure lethargy and psychosomatic paralysis, and scherzos to relieve deep depression or mere laziness.[14] If these commentators are right, it would seem that music does not produce its effects through association alone and that Altshuler's theory of music's neural pathways may be partially correct.

Patients are often encouraged to participate in producing music as well as to listen to it. One practitioner cited the following case history of a nineteen-year-old college student at the C. F. Menninger Memorial Hospital:

> His activity was constant and uncontrollable. The boy had apparently found that only loud and violent activity would attract the love and attention he wanted. Doctors learned that the boy had played piano and clarinet while in elementary school, so they suggested that he take up music again. He agreed to start piano but declared he would play no scales or exercises. He was given tuneful pieces, some with a pounding bass line which he obviously enjoyed. He frequently interrupted his lesson with angry outbursts in which he shouted and threw his books on the floor. He achieved similar results with the clarinet. His playing was erratic, but he insisted on trying pieces too difficult for him. A turning point came when he wanted to play in a combo. Doctors told him the combo was too advanced for him, both in the level of music and in the emotional maturity demanded of members. The boy was so eager to join the group that he did extra practicing and was willing to take orders, control his temper, and cooperate with others. He was accepted in the combo and soon became one of its leaders.[15]

Sometimes, too, patients are encouraged to sing, even just to themselves, in order to alter undesirable moods.[16] Singing apparently distracts the patients, since it serves to shift their attention away from their problems.

In a few cases, music therapy has been used to reach patients who have ceased to respond to anything in their environment.[17] One psychiatrist

A direct quotation that occupies more than six lines is called an inset quotation and is indented five spaces from the margin of the text. Do not enclose an inset quotation in quotation marks.

Inset quotations are discussed on pages 82–84.

---

[14]P. L. Van Auken, "Beethoven: Humanitarian and 'Physician,'" *American Mercury*, Jan. 1961, p. 83.

[15]Winifred D. Hansen, "Music for the Mentally Ill," *Recreation*, 54 (May 1961), 271.

[16]Altshuler, p. 272.

[17]C. J. McNaspy, "Music Therapy," *America*, 112 (8 May 1965), 730.

8

reported that a patient who had neither spoken for several weeks nor shown any recognition of visitors responded to a song that had been popular when he was young. His general improvement was slight but apparently permanent.[18] This case, too, shows that music can evoke responses through association.

Because music has the ability to affect groups as well as individuals, it has been used in group therapy. Alva Cook, then a staff psychiatrist in a Veterans Administration hospital, reported that during one Christmas season a group of mental patients began to sing Christmas carols. Cook was so impressed by the improvement he noted in some patients that he felt such activity should not end with the holiday season. He arranged for singing groups to continue and reported some success. He felt that the music itself was at least partly responsible for the improvement, and he concluded his report by saying "I am convinced that this is a type of experience many of our patients need, and providing this experience would represent a real contribution on the part of music therapists."[19] Cook's report lends weight to Altshuler's theory of the neural pathway of music, and the importance that such a pathway may have in music therapy.

Even senility, which is in a sense a mental illness, though it is also a degenerative disease, can sometimes be slightly abated by music therapy. One commentator reported the case of a "ninety-year-old woman who had lost all contact with reality. Music had little effect until one waltz familiar to her was played. Upon hearing this, she sat up in bed and smiled at the memories it brought back."[20] Unfortunately, the improvement was not permanent. But the case does provide further support for the theory that music produces its effects in part through association.

---

[18]Interview with Joseph P. Mayer at Kern General Hospital, Bakersfield, California, 6 March 1974.

[19]"Remarks," in *Music Therapy 1956*, ed. E. Thayer Gaston (Lawrence, Kansas: The National Association for Music Therapy, 1957), p. 78.

[20]Doris A. Paul, "Delightful Delusion," *Etude*, 73 (June 1955), 46.

Outline heading III.C. has been sufficiently covered in this one unified paragraph; no extraneous material has been introduced in the paragraph.

Refer to pages 86–91 for a discussion of developing unified paragraphs from outline headings.

The student was able to obtain useful information by interviewing someone particularly knowledgeable about the topic.

See page 37 for other suggestions for obtaining first-hand information.

9

The phrasing of the topic sentence of this paragraph tells the reader that outline heading IV will be developed in a unified paragraph. See pages 86–91.

Music therapy has also helped to "resocialize" patients, that is, to induce withdrawn patients to participate in active social relationships. The idea is to involve the withdrawn patient in group music activities-- usually the production of music. Some practitioners claim that not only group activity but the music itself is responsible for withdrawn patients becoming noticeably more social.[21] In music therapy for resocialization, patients learn to cooperate, to take orders, to compete for a position, and, most importantly, to make friends. One case history involved a patient who was uncooperative, uninterested in hospital routine, and generally with- drawn. He was asked several times to join the drum and bugle corps, but each time he refused. Finally, he learned to play drums and became a mem- ber. Once a part of the group his attitude improved. He made new friends, and he was moved from the closed ward to a priviledged ward.[22]

Music therapy has been found effective in treating physical ills, though often a psychological factor is involved as well. As early as 1917, before modern practitioners became interested in music therapy, a man reported that music in minor keys had a soothing effect on his neuritis, whereas music in major keys increased his pain.[23] It could well be that the physical effects of music, such as changing the electrical conductivity of the body or alter- ing muscle contractions, were responsible for this man's relief from pain. This man's experience lends weight to the theory that music's effects are not produced through association alone.

---

[21]Hughes, p. 185.

[22]Art Wrobel, "A Drum and Bugle Corps," _Recreation_, 48 (Oct. 1955), 392.

[23]Soibelman, p. 162.

10

In another case, a woman suffering from a gunshot wound lay for days near death, her pain relieved by drugs. Realization of her situation apparently took away her will to live. Her doctor called in volunteer Red Cross workers, who sometimes use music to relieve depressed hospital patients, and they played the piano outside the patient's door. Soon the patient asked the volunteers to come into her room to play for her. She found that her pain began to diminish without drugs, and she regained the will to live. Later she herself joined the volunteers.[24]

Music therapy has also helped to rehabilitate patients with brain damage. In 1958 Richard Weber invented Musicall, a simplified method of teaching music to brain-damaged patients. Musicall uses familiar tunes containing only six notes, which are written on music paper with letter names printed under them and on piano keys as well. The patient matches the letter on the music to the letter on the keyboard. Musicall as therapy helps to reduce the effects of brain damage.[25]

One of the first experiments with Musicall was conducted with Steve Bell, a fourteen-year-old with severe brain damage. He had trouble with speech, physical coordination, and mental concentration. He was falling behind in school and was becoming withdrawn and moody. He showed an aptitude for music, however, and he started lessons with Weber. Within a year he played in an organ recital and entertained at local parties. His coordination so improved that he was able to drive a car and a tractor. By the time he was twenty, he was self-supporting and was continuing his musical training. Weber explained that Bell's simultaneous use of his body and

---

[24]William S. Dutton, "Why Not Music like This in all Hospitals?" Reader's Digest, Jan. 1956, p. 202.

[25]Evan McLeod Wylie, "Pied Piper from Peoria," Reader's Digest, August 1968, p. 59.

By keeping paragraph length at 75 to 150 words, the student avoids overlong and disunified paragraphs. See pages 86–91.

The material for heading V.B.1. was too extensive for one paragraph; the student used two indentations, with the topic sentence of the first serving both paragraphs. The second indentation comes at a natural breaking point. See pages 86–91.

brain in musical practice improved his coordination and concentration.[26]

Patients with other physical handicaps due to brain damage have been helped by music therapy. In many cases, muscles of brain-damaged patients need to be reeducated. Therapists sometimes undertake this reeducation by having patients practice in specified ways on various instruments, concentrating on rhythm. Some success in this kind of therapy has been reported.[27] For example, when polio was a common disease, some children afflicted by it regained muscle coordination by performing physical actions in conjunction with musical rhythm. One nine-year-old victim could not even make a pencil mark on paper unless someone guided her hand. After two years of music therapy she could play chords with either hand while the other hand played the melody.[28] Another polio victim was able to dispense with arm supports after four months of music therapy.[29] With such success with polio victims, it seems reasonable to assume that other physical disabilities affecting muscles might respond to music therapy.

Music therapy, then, seems to have had many successes. It has been shown to be effective, in some cases, in calming disturbed patients, in altering undesirable moods, and in resocializing withdrawn patients. It has had some success in the retraining of injured muscles and in improving the performance of patients with brain damage. But still it is not in widespread use. One psychiatrist who experimented with various kinds of music therapy asserts that "music does not have special therapeutic qualities. The suc-

---

[26]Ibid., p. 60

[27]Ibid., p. 62.

[28]Wylie, p. 60.

[29]Gerald McGeorge, "Piano for the Hand-de-Capped," _Etude_, 73 (May 1955), 59.

The student begins the conclusion by summarizing the successes of music therapy.
Since the material for heading VI is too extensive for one paragraph, the student has begun new paragraphs at natural breaking points.

See pages 96–97 for a discussion on writing the conclusion.

12

cesses reported for it would for the most part have been successes with some other activity substituted for music."[30] This practitioner concedes, however, that music is often as effective as any other activity in producing successful psychotherapy, and thus urges that both experimentation in and practical application of music therapy be continued.

Another doctor maintains that music itself is not therapeutic but that it helps the patient to utilize other therapeutic services through its effect on mood and behavior.[31] This would seem to be only a technical distinction, since the music is participating in the therapy. The doctor who made this claim, however, also maintains that various activities besides music are as effective as music in helping a patient utilize other therapeutic services.

The present trend in music therapy seems to be a continuation of only a modest amount of practical music therapy and a modest amount of experimentation in it. Since about 1965 there has been a noticeable decline in the number of published articles on the therapeutic uses of music, which might be evidence that music therapy is not especially successful and is on the wane. Still, some practitioners are optimistic about its future, believing that it will eventually become a major tool in psychiatric treatment and in physical rehabilitation.[32]

------

[30]George Morton, "Music in Therapy," <u>Physics Health,</u> June 1970, p. 39.

[31]Hansen, p. 271.

[32]Alvin, pp. 160–61.

From reading these concluding paragraphs, a reader can guess rather closely what the text of the paper has said. The reader also *feels* the completion of the paper.

13

BIBLIOGRAPHY

Altshuler, Ira. M. "A Psychiatrist's Experience with Music as a Therapeutic Agent." Music and Medicine. Ed. Dorothy A. Schullian and Max Schoen. New York: Henry Schuman, 1948. Pp. 269-74.

Alvin, Juliette. Music Therapy. New York: Humanities Press, 1966.

Beavers, S. V. "Hospital Music Clinic." Recreation, 56 (Dec. 1963), 479.

Cook, Alva. "Remarks." Music Therapy 1956. Ed. E. Thayer Gaston. Lawrence, Kansas: The National Association for Music Therapy, 1957. Pp. 77-78.

Diserens, Charles M. "The Development of an Experimental Psychology of Music." Music and Medicine. Ed. Dorothy A. Schullian and Max Schoen. New York: Henry Schuman, 1948. Pp. 380-85.

Dutton, William S. "Why Not Music like This in All Hospitals?" Reader's Digest, Jan. 1956, pp. 197-202.

Fowler, Charles. "The Noise That Banishes Pain." Popular Electronics, Jan. 1961, p. 50.

Hansen, Winifred D. "Music for the Mentally Ill." Recreation, 54 (May 1961), 271-72.

Hughes, Charles W. "Rhythm and Health." Music and Medicine. Ed. Dorothy A. Schullian and Max Schoen. New York: Henry Schuman, 1948. Pp. 184-87.

Interview with Joseph P. Mayer, Psychiatrist, Kern General Hospital, Bakersfield, Calif., 6 March 1974.

McGeorge, Gerald. "Piano for the Hand-de-Capped." Etude, 73 (May 1955), 26 ff.

McNaspy, C. J. "Music Therapy." America, 112 (8 May 1965), 730-31.

Morton, George. "Music in Therapy." Physics Health, June 1970, pp. 38-41.

"Music Not to Listen To." In "After Hours." Harper's, Nov. 1956, pp. 81-82.

Paul, Doris A. "Delightful Delusion." Etude, 73 (June 1955), 45-46.

Soibelman, Doris. Therapeutic and Industrial Uses of Music. New York: Columbia Univ. Press, 1948.

Van Auken, P. L. "Beethoven: Humanitarian and 'Physician.'" American Mercury, Jan. 1961, pp. 82-83.

Wrobel, Art. "A Drum and Bugle Corps." Recreation, 48 (Oct. 1955), 392-93.

Wylie, Evan McLeod. "Pied Piper from Peoria." Reader's Digest, August 1968, pp. 58-62.

Refer to bibliographic forms on pages 68–70 to be sure that your entries contain the necessary information and follow the proper form.

For instructions on typing the bibliography, see page 100.

The comments in the margins point out aspects of term-paper writing described in the textbook.

The Red Badge of Courage as a Naturalistic Novel

by Joseph Vasquez

See page 98 for instructions on composing and typing the title page.

English 30B

American Literature Since 1865

Professor Alan Wardner

May 21, 1975

1

Even though you
have a separate
title page, the title
of your paper
should be repeated
at the top of the
outline page.

For instructions on
typing the formal
outline, see page
99.

This outline is a
topic outline; see
page 72 for an ex-
ample of a sen-
tence outline.

See Chapter 8 (p.
71) for a discus-
sion on writing the
formal outline.

<u>The Red Badge of Courage</u> as a Naturalistic Novel

Outline

I. Critical Reception of <u>The Red Badge of Courage</u>

    A. Critical praise it has received

    B. Contradictory interpretations of its meaning

II. Two allegorical interpretations of the novel

    A. Stallman's interpretation of it as Christian allegory

    B. Hart's interpretation of it as myth

III. A brief definition of the philosophy of naturalism

IV. The philosophy of naturalism in some of Crane's other works

    A. In his short stories

    B. In his poetry

V. The philosophy of naturalism in <u>The Red Badge of Courage</u>

    A. Henry Fleming's conditioned response to war fever

    B. The soldiers' response to circumstances they do not understand

    C. Henry's random and contradictory behavior

    D. The confusion of battle as a symbol of naturalism

    E. The unpredictability of Henry's flight from battle

    F. The naturalistic circumstances of Henry's bravery in the final

       battle in the novel

2

<u>The Red Badge of Courage</u> as a Naturalistic Novel

With the exception of a very few early negative reviews, Stephen Crane's

<u>The Red Badge of Courage</u> (1895) has received continuously high critical

praise.[1] One early reviewer wrote "Mr. Stephen Crane . . . is a great ar-

tist, with something new to say, and consequently, with a new way of saying

it."[2] Other critics have praised his novel's amazing accuracy in portraying

soldiers in battle and its rich impressionistic (or realistic or naturalis-

tic) style.[3] The novel has probably been discussed more and held in higher

esteem than any other American war novel.

But, like most literary works of great richness, <u>The Red Badge</u> has re-

ceived sharply contradictory interpretations. Charles Child Walcutt said

the book

> . . . is the most controversial piece in his [Crane's] canon. It has
> been much discussed and most variously interpreted, and the inter-
> pretations range about as widely as they could. Is it a Christian
> story of redemption? Is it a demonstration that man is a beast with
> illusions? Or is it, between these extremes, the story of a man who
> goes through fire, discovers himself, and with the self-knowledge that
> he is able to attain comes to terms with the problems of life insofar
> as an imperfect man can come to terms with an imperfect world?[4]

There are two basic interpretations of the novel; one is allegorical,

the other symbolic. The best known is Robert Wooster Stallman's interpre-

tation of the novel as an allegory of the Christian belief in rebirth and

redemption.[5] Stallman maintains that Henry Fleming, the novel's main char-

acter, achieves salvation through the spiritual growth resulting from his

war experiences. Stallman cites as evidence some Biblical phrasing in the

novel, Henry's slow spiritual change, and Henry's flag as a representation

of his conscience.[6] Stallman also sees Henry's conscience as symbolized by

"the forest, the cathedral-forest where Henry retreats to nurse his guilt-

wound . . . ."[7]

Three spaced periods (ellipsis points) indicate an omission in the interior of a sentence of a direct quotation.

The introduction leads the reader directly into the subject matter of the paper; the tone and style engage the reader's inter- est.

See pages 80–82 for a discussion on writing the intro- duction.

After the first refer- ence, titles of works mentioned frequently in the text should be shortened.

Use brackets to en- close comments or explanations in- serted in quoted material.

When all footnotes are at the end of the paper, always include the author's name in the footnote even if it has been used in the footnoted passage. See foot- note 5 on page 10 of this paper.

3

The most surprising evidence that Stallman presents is his interpretation of the role that Henry's friend Jim Conklin plays in the novel. Stallman contends that "Henry's regeneration is brought about by the death of Jim Conklin," and that Conklin's initials--J. C.--and the wound in his side show that Crane intended Conklin to represent Jesus Christ. When Conklin dies, Henry is reborn, and the Christian allegory is completed.[8]

John E. Hart sees <u>The Red Badge</u> as only superficially realistic. He maintains that the novel's "moral and meaning, its reliance on symbol follow in detail the traditional formula of myth."[9] According to Hart, rites and revelations transform Henry Fleming so that he comes to identify himself with his comrades. The surface story of men in battle, Hart maintains, is relevant only in that it is a vehicle to carry the symbols that fashion the myth--the true meaning of the novel.[10]

The allegorical and symbolic interpretations of <u>The Red Badge</u> are interesting but seem wide of the mark. Crane's novel is a realistic narrative of events which show that Crane was influenced by the philosophy of naturalism. The philosophy of naturalism maintains that all species, including human beings, are governed by the same physical, chemical, and biological natural laws. Humans, this philosophy maintains, have little control over what they are and the direction that their lives take. They react naturally to their environment, thinking that they are exercising free will only because their view of the world is so limited. People are victims of circumstances that they do not understand. No supernaturalism touches them; they are bound by natural laws as much as any tick or tiger.[11]

That Stephen Crane was influenced by the philosophy of naturalism is evident in many of his other works. Many of Crane's short stories, for example, are undeniably naturalistic. The theme of "The Open Boat," a story based on personal experience, is that people are irrationally buffeted about

The phrasing of the topic sentence of this paragraph tells the reader that outline heading IV will be developed in a unified paragraph.

Refer to pages 86–91 for a discussion on developing unified paragraphs from outline headings.

4

by life and have little control over what happens to them. A bit of dialogue
repeated several times in the story--"if I am going to be drowned, why, in
the name of the seven mad gods who rule the sea, was I allowed to come thus
far and contemplate sand and trees?"[12]--clearly implies that there is no order or rationality in life, that natural law rules everything.

"The Bride Comes to Yellow Sky" shows a man and woman who assume they
are exercising their free wills, but who are in reality passively yielding
to their fate. In "The Monster," people are shown to be inexorably controlled by circumstances they don't understand. The story entitled "The
Blue Hotel" not only implies naturalism in its flow of events but even has a
character who openly expresses the philosophy. In discussing a murder that
occurred earlier in the story, a character called the Easterner says, "We
are all in it. This poor gambler [the murderer] isn't even a noun. He is
kind of an adverb. Every sin is the result of a collaboration." The rest
of the Easterner's speech points out that people live in a tangled web without understanding why things happen to them or what they unknowingly do to
others.[13]

Crane's verse expresses the philosophy of naturalism, too. One poem
illustrates perfectly his scientific, naturalistic view of man:[14]

> A man said to the universe:
> "Sir, I exist!"
> "However," replied the universe,
> "The fact has not created in me
> A sense of obligation."[15]

Because the influence of naturalism on Crane's other work was so strong,
it seems reasonable to inquire whether The Red Badge expresses a similar
philosophy. Such an inquiry is especially valid in view of what Crane wrote
about The Red Badge in a letter to John Hilliard: "My chieftest [sic] desire was to write plainly and unmistakably, so that all . . . might read and
understand."[16] Crane believed that if a story is told in its actuality--as

When the number
of lines of poetry
quoted runs to four
or more, they
should be entered
as an inset and
footnoted in the
regular way.

Inset quotations
are discussed on
pages 82–84.

Here the student
begins to present
his own interpreta-
tion of *The Red
Badge of Courage*.

Sic, placed in
brackets, indicates
that a passage con-
taining an unusual
spelling, an error,
or some startling in-
formation has been
quoted accurately.

5

it would happen in real life--it will convey its own "interpretive comment"
without the necessity of direct statement by the author.[17] Though Crane
does not make direct comments to the effect that Henry Fleming is carried
along in life like a piece of bark tumbling down a rushing stream, the story
speaks that view.

A short flashback in the opening chapter of The Red Badge presents
Henry as a youth who enlists in the Union Army not because he is following a
carefully thought-out plan or a genuine feeling of patriotism, but simply
because he is drawn along by events that he understands only in the vaguest
way. Henry's simple announcement, "Ma, I've enlisted," and his mother's
fatalistic reply, "The Lord's will be done, Henry,"[18] are an effective con-
trast to the excitement Henry experiences at the thought of enlistment and
of marching into battle--excitement which his life has conditioned him to
feel. In Chapter 1, Henry is portrayed as a human being who, although he
thinks of himself as making reasoned decisions, is really responding to his
environment in a conditioned way.

Although Henry's sudden "panic-fear" of running from battle might be
taken as evidence that he is fully aware of himself and of his total environment, it is clear that Crane intends his readers to understand that
Henry's sudden concern is an inevitable consequence of the circumstances he
is in. Significantly, this passage accompanies Henry's thoughts on running
from battle: "In his life he had taken certain things for granted, never
challenging his belief in ultimate success, and bothering little about means
and roads. But here he was confronted with a thing of moment."[19] Here we
see Henry portrayed as a being who follows the course of the stream, aware
of sudden shifts but reacting not as a person exercising full free will but
as a person propelled by circumstance. After Henry discusses with his
friends the possibility of running from battle, Crane writes that "he was

Throughout his in-
terpretation, the
student uses direct
quotations to em-
phasize and sup-
port important
points.

Uses of direct quo-
tation are dis-
cussed on pages
82–84.

6

compelled to sink back into his old place as part of a blue demonstration."[20]

As the soldiers in Henry's outfit wait for battle and speculate end-
lessly on what will happen and when it will happen, they are presented not
as allegorical characters or mythic heroes but as beings controlled by circumstances that they only dimly perceive. They bluster and joke and pretend
to a firm understanding of what is occurring and what will occur, but Crane's
narrative conveys their ignorance of their destiny and their blind response
to the circumstances surrounding them. Henry can't understand their aimless
bluster, for he is obsessed with his fear of running. Crane is showing the
randomness of the behavior of people cast into roles that they have not spe-
cifically chosen for themselves. He is suggesting the web of circumstance
that is part of the naturalist's philosophy when he writes that [Henry's]
"failure to discover any mite of resemblance in their view points made him
more miserable than before."[21]

As Henry advances with his comrades toward what they think will be
battle, his thoughts shift rapidly and randomly. He feels that he is trap-
ped by a mob. Then he feels that he must warn his comrades. He persuades
himself that he did not enlist of his own free will. Absurd ideas take hold
of him. Hatred for generals and compassion for his comrades flow through
his mind. He lags. Then he is overtaken by a fever of impatience.[22] Here
Crane is presenting a naturalistic view of human nature and human behavior.
Henry is a victim of circumstances he does not understand.

The general confusion surrounding the troops in battle is interpreted
by Stallman as allegorical--Henry loses his soul in the midst of the turmoil;
rebirth and redemption will follow.[23] A sounder interpretation, it would
seem, is that the confusion, the contradictory behavior of some of the soldiers, and the apparent aimlessness of it all are symbolic of a person's
lack of understanding of the nature of life. Crane seems to be saying that

The student has avoided overlong and disunified paragraphs by keeping paragraph length at 75 to 100 words.

See pages 86–91 for a discussion of developing unified paragraphs.

The material for outline heading V.D. was too extensive to be covered in one paragraph. The student has used three indentations, with the second and third beginning at natural breaking points where a smooth transition can be made from one paragraph to another.

sample term papers

the bewilderment and disorientation of battle are a supreme example of the directionlessness of human life. Individuals think they are guiding their own lives only because they can see and understand so little. When Crane writes "It was surprising that Nature had gone tranquilly on with her golden process in the midst of so much devilment,"[24] he is saying that the chaos of battle is just an aspect of the naturalistic order of things.

That Henry goes through a battle, conducts himself with some show of bravery, and is happy that "it" is over at last, only later to bolt and run like a coward, is meant to illustrate the minimal control that people have over their progress through life. Henry is not pursuing a premeditated route to salvation but is simply moving in one direction until some circumstance causes him to change directions. He thinks he is guiding his life because he sees so little of the vastly complicated circumstances surrounding him.

Henry's flight from battle can only be interpreted as symbolic of naturalism's contention that people have little if any control over their role in life. The words Crane uses demonstrate this: "He ran like a blind man . . . . His fears had been wondrously magnified . . . . The noises of the battle were like stones . . . . What manner of men were they, anyhow?"[25] These phrases seem to imply that Henry was caught up in circumstances beyond his control, not that he was going through a process of rebirth and redemption. He is behaving as a member of a biological species, not as a being possessed with transcendent spirit.

The allegorists see Henry's undetected flight and his heroic advance as flag bearer in the next battle as symbolic of his spiritual change and his achievement of salvation.[26] A more valid interpretation is that Henry is living a naturalistic life of chance and circumstance. Once he sees that his flight and his supposed war wound have not been and will not be detected,

---

Three unified paragraphs have covered outline heading V.D.

Throughout the paper the student has achieved coherence by the use of connectives, repetition of key words, and use of pronoun reference.

8

"He had license to be pompous and veteranlike."[27] He begins to build fantasies about himself--he is "chosen of gods and doomed to greatness."[28] He feels scorn for many of the other soldiers. Although fears that his cowardice might be detected surface occasionally, he is essentially dishonest in his acceptance of praise. Surely such behavior as this cannot be interpreted as myth or ritual redemption.

Henry's seizure of the colors and his brave action as standard bearer are not symbolic of his new spiritual state. He goes recklessly into battle and amazes his comrades because he resents the contempt that the general and colonel have expressed for his unit. As his behavior is described, references to his anger are numerous. "We <u>are</u> mule drivers, are we?"[29] he mutters at one point and keeps the flag erect to show his resentment of the officers' comments. In short, Crane is showing that certain circumstances can cause people to reverse their behavior. The praise that Henry finally receives from the officers for his brave stand is just a circumstance that alters Henry. Naturally he has changed a good deal because of his experiences, but the changes are not God-wrought but due to circumstances which are not of Henry's conscious creation.

At the end of the novel, Henry is "gleeful" because "his public deeds were paraded in great and shining prominence." But "Nevertheless, the ghost of his flight from the first engagement appeared to him and danced. There were small shoutings in his brain about these matters."[30] Henry is simply a naturalistic being. He glories in his fine performance and the praise he received, but he is anxious about the possibility that his shame might be exposed. Crane's story illustrates the naturalistic philosophy that humans are a species subject to natural laws and life amid circumstances that they understand dimly, if at all. Henry and the other soldiers react as natural law dictates, not as though they are guided by a deity providing them with

See pages 91–94 for a discussion on maintaining coherence between and within paragraphs.

The concluding paragraph should not review all the details of the paper, but it should summarize any overall conclusion the student has drawn, even if that conclusion has been made clear in the paper.

See pages 96–97 for a discussion on writing the conclusion.

redemption and salvation, but as imperfect beings in an imperfect, unpredictable, and largely incomprehensible world.

10

Footnotes

[1]Nancy H. Banks, "The Novel of a Journalist," _Bookman_, 2 (Nov. 1895), 217-20. A. C. McClurg, "The Red Badge of Hysteria," _Dial_, 20 (16 April 1896), 226-29.

[2]George Wyndham, "A Remarkable Book," _New Review_, Jan. 1896, p. 32.

[3]M. Solomon, "Stephen Crane: A Critical Study," _Mainstream_, Jan. 1956, p. 38.

[4]Charles Child Walcutt, _American Literary Naturalism, a Divided Stream_ (Minneapolis: Univ. of Minn. Press, 1956), p. 75.

[5]Robert Wooster Stallman, ed., _The Red Badge of Courage by Stephen Crane_ (New York: Random House, 1951), pp. xxii-xxxv.

[6]Ibid., passim.

[7]Ibid., p. xxxi.

[8]Ibid., pp. xxxiii-xxxiv.

[9]John E. Hart, "_The Red Badge of Courage_ as Myth and Symbol," _Univ. of Kansas City Review_, 19 (Summer 1953), 249.

[10]Ibid.

[11]Scully Bradley et al., eds., _The American Tradition in Literature_, vol. 2, 3rd ed. (New York: Norton, 1967), pp. 941-42.

[12]Thomas A. Gullason, ed., _The Complete Short Stories and Sketches of Stephen Crane_ (New York: Doubleday, 1963), p. 350.

[13]Ibid., pp. 506-07.

[14]This poem appeared in Crane's second book of verse, _War Is Kind_ (1899). The poem is untitled, as were all of Crane's poems.

[15]Bradley, p. 946.

[16]Richard Lettis et al., eds., _Stephen Crane's The Red Badge of Courage_ (New York: Harcourt Brace Jovanovich, Inc., 1960), p. 90.

[17]Bradley, p. 941.

[18]Stephen Crane, _The Red Badge of Courage_, ed. Max J. Herzburg (New York: Appleton-Century-Crofts, 1954), p. 7.

[19]Ibid., p. 13.

[20]Ibid., p. 18.

See page 99 for instructions on how to enter footnotes at the end of the paper.

Refer to footnote forms on pages 63-66 to be sure that your footnotes contain the necessary information and follow the proper form.

Short forms for subsequent references are described on pages 66-67.

Footnote 14 is an explanatory footnote containing information that would be out of place in the text of the paper.

11

[21]Ibid., p. 30.

[22]Ibid., pp. 35–43.

[23]Stallman, p. xxxiii.

[24]Crane, p. 63.

[25]Ibid., pp. 69–72.

[26]Stallman, p. xxxiii.

[27]Crane, p. 150.

[28]Ibid., p. 151.

[29]Ibid., p. 192.

[30]Ibid., p. 229.

12

Bibliography

Banks, Nancy H. "The Novel of a Journalist." <u>Bookman</u>, 2 (Nov. 1895), 217-20.

Bradley, Scully et al, eds. <u>The American Tradition in Literature</u>. Vol. 2, 3rd ed. New York: Norton, 1967.

Crane, Stephen. <u>The Red Badge of Courage</u>. Ed. Max J. Herzburg. New York: Appleton-Century-Crofts, 1954.

-------------- <u>The Red Badge of Courage</u>. Ed. Robert Wooster Stallman. New York: Random House, 1951.

Gullason, Thomas A., ed. <u>The Complete Short Stories and Sketches of Stephen Crane</u>. New York: Doubleday, 1963.

Hart, John E. "<u>The Red Badge of Courage</u> as Myth and Symbol." <u>Univ. of Kansas City Review</u>, 19 (summer 1953), 249-56.

Lettis, Richard et al., eds. <u>Stephen Crane's The Red Badge of Courage</u>. New York: Harcourt Brace Jovanovich, Inc., 1960.

McClurg, A. C. "The Red Badge of Hysteria." <u>Dial</u>, 20 (16 April 1896), 226-29.

Solomon, M. "Stephen Crane: A Critical Study." <u>Mainstream</u>, Jan. 1956, pp. 25-42.

Walcutt, Charles Child. <u>American Literary Naturalism, a Divided Stream</u>. Minneapolis: Univ. of Minn. Press, 1956.

Wyndham, George. "A Remarkable Book." <u>New Review</u>, Jan. 1896, pp. 32-40.

Refer to bibliographic forms on pages 68–70 to be sure that your entries contain the necessary information and follow the proper form.

For instructions on typing the bibliography, see page 100.

appendix: writing and documenting the scientific term paper

In preparing a scientific term paper you will use many of the aspects of term-paper writing discussed in previous chapters. As you will discover in this appendix, however, writing and documenting a scientific term paper requires the mastery of several additional techniques.

THE SCIENTIFIC APPROACH

Scientific method requires that findings from any experiment or research work may be replicated—repeated or duplicated—under the same conditions and circumstances by anyone and that such findings

132   will be identical no matter who performs the experiment. Scientists who want their theses to be credible have developed a meticulous approach to their work and research. This approach has three indispensable characteristics that you should learn to apply in writing your scientific paper: objectivity, neutrality, and observation.

Objectivity requires researchers or experimenters to remove themselves from the conditions of the experiment; that is, they must not permit their feelings, opinions, expectations, and preconceived notions to influence the conduct or results of the research. Judgments and interpretations must be kept separate and, when expressed in a paper, clearly labeled as such.

Neutrality requires researchers to maintain an open mind until their research is complete. If findings fail to support a hypothesis the researcher favors, a change of mind and a corresponding adjustment in hypothesis is clearly necessary. Openmindedness is essential to the credibility of any scientific research.

Observation requires researchers to assume nothing, to take for granted nothing about their topic. Information presented in a scientific paper is derived from factual data, which is used either to develop or to support a thesis or argument. Conclusions are valid only if they can be supported by data. Do not force data to back up opinions; do not adjust findings to support preconceived notions.

By maintaining these three attitudes—objectivity, neutrality, and strictness in observation—you will be able to write a credible and acceptable scientific term paper, whatever your topic or discipline.

AVOIDING STYLISTIC PITFALLS

Although scientific papers are noteworthy for their strict adherence to scientific detachment, such detachment can lead to writing problems. One problem common in scientific writing is the overuse of the passive voice. Temptation to use the passive voice arises from its quality of enhancing the sense of detachment, which permits scientific writers to appear uninvolved with what they are reporting. Yet overuse of the passive voice often produces writing that lacks emphasis and vigor.

Among scientists who read one another's writings, the use of jargon is not a problem; every discipline has its own special and technical vocabulary. But scientific writers should be certain that readers understand the vocabulary they use and are therefore well advised to keep jargon to a minimum. For additional suggestions on how to write your paper, see Chapter 9.

One further point: most writing for the sciences consists of reports

of experiments or of compilations of findings from several experiments. **133**
Unlike writing in research and critical papers, scientific writing is characterized by the inclusion of much hard data, usually in the form of
tables or graphs. (Refer to pages 94–96 for instructions on entering
tables and other illustrations in your term paper.) Occasionally you will
include generalizations that do not arise from these data, but you will
rarely, if ever, pass judgment on your findings. Remember that your
paper is not a vehicle for the expression of your feelings. Maintain a scientific attitude toward your topic, and remember that your conclusions
must stem from your observations. You cannot select only those data
that support preconceived notions and ignore findings to the contrary.

DOCUMENTATION

In preparing your scientific term paper, you will consult various sources:
encyclopedias, books, journals, magazines, newspapers, and unpublished theses and dissertations. Review the procedures described in
Chapters 3 through 8 as you assemble your information.

Conventions for documenting the sources listed above vary from
discipline to discipline. At the end of this appendix sample reference
lists illustrate appropriate forms for various disciplines. You will discover, for example, that some disciplines omit the title of an article on
the grounds that the author's name, journal title, volume number, year,
and page numbers provide sufficient information. Other disciplines
prefer to include and italicize journal titles, and some place the date of
publication before the page numbers rather than after. Record these
variations in form on your bibliography cards as you do your research.
Even though many of the variations are minor, they must be observed
and respected.

Although different disciplines often follow different forms for the
listing of references, there are some general rules for documentation
that most disciplines follow.

Many scientific papers require no footnotes other than those that
explain or expand upon an item of content. In the text of your paper insert a number that refers to an entry in the reference list:

According to Smith and Peterson (1), . . .

or to a year of publication:

According to Smith and Peterson (1974), . . .

134   These two methods should be adequate for documentating your paper in nearly every discipline. The purpose of the inserts is to indicate the sources of your data, which are listed in the bibliography at the end of your paper. The word *bibliography,* however, is seldom used as the heading for this list of source materials. Most disciplines use such headings as "Literature Cited," "List of References," or simply "References." Although there are minor variations in form for listing source materials, most scientific papers share the following conventions:

Capitalize only the first word of the title of a book or article, for example:

> Smith, P., and K. Peterson, Occupational status in the printing and publishing industry . . .

In general, abbreviate names of periodicals:

> *Journal of the American Chemical Society* becomes *J. Amer. Chem. Soc.,* 88

For psychology and sociology, however, names must be spelled out in full:

> *Psychological Review,* 1963, 70
> *American Sociological Review,* 18

Notice that the volume numbers of journals appear in arabic numerals and that some disciplines require italics or the abbreviation *vol.* for the volume number. Consult the lists at the end of this appendix for the proper forms for each discipline.

Reference Entries in the Text of Your Paper

The formal list of references at the end of your paper may or may not be alphabetized, depending on the discipline. If you are using the number system for documenting your sources, you will have to assign a number to each entry. Even if several entries are written by the same author, each entry must be given a separate number. The numbering system often follows the sequence in which the references appear in the text, regardless of the alphabetical order of authors' names. Sometimes, however, names are listed alphabetically and are numbered consecutively despite the order of their appearance in the text. The list below illustrates documentation for a biology paper. Note that the list is both numbered and alphabetized.

> 1. Davis, A. 1970. Let's eat right to keep fit. Harcourt Brace Jovanovich, N.Y.

2. Johnston, E. M. Maternal and infant nutrition attitudes and practices of physicians in British Columbia. Ph.D. dissertation, The University of British Columbia (Canada), 1975.
3. Manocha, Sohan L. 1974. Nutrition and our overpopulated planet. Charles C. Thomas, Publisher, Springfield, Ill.
4. Schroeder, Henry A., and Marian Mitchener. 1975. Lifeterm effects of mercury, methyl mercury, and nine other trace metals on mice. *J. Nutr. 105* (4): 452.
5. Scriver, C. R., and L. E. Rosenberg. 1973. Amino acid metabolism and its disorders. *In:* Major Problems in Clinical Pediatrics, Vol. X (A. L. Schaffer, consulting ed.) W. B. Saunders Co., Philadelphia, pp. 256–289.

In the text of the paper insert the number, enclosed in parentheses, after the name of the authority you are citing:

> According to Schroeder and Mitchener (4), previous research has yielded conflicting findings that appear to be equally valid.

To document a reference when the author's name does not appear in the text of your paper, enclose both the author's name and the entry number in parentheses:

> According to Johnston (2) previous research (Davis, 1, Manocha, 3, and Scriver and Rosenberg, 5) has yielded conflicting findings that appear to be equally valid.

Some disciplines require brackets as well as parentheses for such situations:

> . . . previous research (Davis [1], Manocha [3], and Scriver and Rosenberg [5] has yielded . . .

Others may require only the number in parentheses:

> . . . previous research (1, 3, 5) has yielded . . .

Additional data may be required, such as specific page numbers:

> According to Johnston (2, p. 65), . . .

As mentioned throughout this appendix, these forms and styles vary considerably among disciplines. But the examples above offer a representative sampling of what you may expect will be required of you in using the number system.

136 The name-and-year method requires you to place the year of publication in parentheses immediately after the author's name:

According to Johnston (1975), . . .

If the author's name does not appear in your text, your entry will show both the name and the year in parentheses:

According to Johnston (1975), previous research (Davis, 1970, Manocha, 1974, and Scriver and Rosenberg, 1973) has yielded . . .

As in the number method, sometimes specific data must be added:

According to Johnston (1975, p. 65), . . .

Occasionally you will cite two or more sources by the same author published in the same year. Simply add a lower-case letter (1966a, 1966b) to distinguish the separate works.

Reference Forms

The reference forms for the various disciplines below illustrate sources you are likely to use in writing a scientific paper. You will probably find it more convenient to refer to the required form each time you write an entry than to try to memorize all the forms.

ANTHROPOLOGY

Cambel, Halet, and R. J. Braidwood
1970 "An Early Farming Village in Turkey." *Scientific American* 222 (March): 50–56.
Hazard, Thomas
1960 "On the Nature of the Numaym and its Counterparts Elsewhere on the Northwest Coast." Paper presented to the 127th Annual Meeting of the Advancement of Science, Denver.
Mead, Margaret
1949 *Male and Female.* New York: Morrow.
1950 *Sex and Temperment in Three Primitive Societies.* New York: Mentor.
1970 *Culture and Commitment.* Garden City: Natural History Press.
Smith, Philip
1972a *The Consequences of Food Production.* Reading, (Mass.): Addison-Wesley.
1972b "Land Use, Settlement Patterns, and Subsis-

tence Agriculture." In *Man, Settlement, and Urbanism*, P. J. Ucko, R. Tringham, and G. W. Dimbleby, eds., pp. 409–425. Cambridge (Mass.): Schenkman.

BIOLOGY

1. Smith, M. H., J. B. Gentry, and J. Pinder. 1974. Annual fluctuations in small mammal population in an eastern hardwood forest. *J. Mammal.* 55 (1): 231–234.
2. Bowsher, David. 1975. Introduction to the anatomy and physiology of the nervous system. 3rd ed. Blackwell Scientific Publications, Oxford, England.
3. Dunson, William A. 1975. The biology of sea snakes. University Park Press, Baltimore, Md.

CHEMISTRY

Anders, M. W., and Latorre, J. P., *J. Chromatogr.*, 55, 409 (1971).

Emeleus, H. J., and Sharpe, A. G., Modern Aspects of Inorganic Chemistry, 4th ed., John Wiley & Sons, New York, N.Y., 1973.

Platt, T., Files, J. G., and Weber, K., *J. Biol. Chem.*, 248, 110 (1973).

MATHEMATICS

1. C. Chevalley, *The theory of lie books I*, Princeton University Press, Princeton, N.J., 1946.
2. R. H. Crowell, *On the Van Kampen theorem*, Pacific J. Math. 9 (1959), 43–50.
3. P. J. Hilton and S. Wylie, *Homology theory, an introduction to algebraic topology*, The University Press, Cambridge, Mass., 1960.
4. I. Richards, *On the classification of noncompact surfaces*, Trans. Am. Math. Soc. *106* (1963), 259–269.

PHYSICS

1. E. W. Lee, *Magnetism* (Penguin Books, Inc., Baltimore, 1963).
2. E. B. Sparburg, "Misinterpretation of Theories of Light," *Am. J. Phys. 34*, 377 (1966).

PSYCHOLOGY

Aaronson, B., and Osmond, H. (eds.) (1970) *Psychedelics: The uses and implications of hallucinogenic drugs.* Garden City, N.Y.: Doubleday.

Blum, G. S. (1966) *Psychodynamics: The science of unconscious mental forces.* Belmont, Calif.: Wadsworth.

138   Funkenstein, D. H. (1955) The physiology of fear and anger. *Scientific American,* 192: 74–80.

Hilgard, E. R. (1961) Hypnosis and experimental psychodynamics. In Brosen, H. (ed.) *Lectures on experimental psychiatry.* Pittsburgh: Univ. of Pittsburgh Press.

Thiessen, D. D., and McGaugh, J. L. (1958) Conflict and curiosity in the rat. Paper, Western Psychological Association, Monterey, Calif.

index

E 9
F 0
G 1
H 2
I 3
J 4
   5